# Sheffielder

## A Life in the City

George Shaw

ALAN SUTTON

First published in the United Kingdom in 1993 by
Alan Sutton Publishing Limited
Phoenix Mill · Far Thrupp · Stroud · Gloucestershire

First published in the United States of America in 1993 by
Alan Sutton Publishing Inc · 83 Washington Street · Dover · NH 03820

British Library Cataloguing in Publication Data
A catalogue record for this book is available from the British Library

ISBN 0 7509 0433 X


Library of Congress Cataloging in Publication Data applied for

*Dedicated to Sally*
*The light at the end of the tunnel*

Typeset in 11/12 Bembo.
Typesetting and origination by
Alan Sutton Publishing Limited.
Printed in Great Britain by
The Bath Press, Avon.

# CONTENTS

# FOREWORD

The temptation to quote Gray's 'Elegy' is irresistible. For George Shaw – as well as recording the 'short and simple annals of the poor' – has demonstrated the continuing growth of literary flowers which are 'born to blush unseen'. Fortunately, the author, at the age of eighty, has decided to remain 'mute and inglorious' no longer. As a result he has produced a fascinating account of life and hard times in the industrial north.

*Sheffielder* does not aspire to be a second *Ragged Trousered Philanthropist*. It preaches no sermons. Nor has it anything in common with *The Diary of a Nobody*, for it does not set out to make readers laugh. But to me at least, the moral and the message are both clear, and they are reinforced by the unselfconscious humour with which the conditions of the working class between the wars is described. Society was, and to a degree still is, organized in a way which wastes its most precious asset – the talents of its people.

George Shaw's chronicles are written with a remarkable objectivity, very little self pity and a total absence of resentment that, because of the class and conditions into which he was born, his creative instinct was stifled for so long. He is living proof that what politicians call 'the politics of envy' is a myth invented by the rich and powerful to combat the calls for justice. George Shaw accepts the station to which he was called with something approaching resignation. He writes of hardship not injustice. If he has any pronounced political allegiance, he does not declare it.

To him, the early summer of 1945 was more notable for the return of the stirrup-pump which he had used as an air-raid warden than for the election of a Labour government. But the strength of *Sheffielder* is that he attempts neither to be didactic nor to provide a guide to the great events of the time. It is the story of the humble and the meek. I have no doubt that during the autumn of 1945 he really was more concerned with the septic ulcers on his mother's legs than he was with the performance of Britain's first majority socialist administration. If he had pretended otherwise, *Sheffielder* would have lost the authenticity which provides so much of its charm.

The feeling of authenticity is enhanced by what, as some early chapters were composed, must have been painful frankness. We are told, right at the beginning of the book, that George Shaw's parents had a brief and stormy marriage which ended soon after their only son was born. And that son – whose admiration for his mother's selfless devotion is almost unqualified – explains that the family's domination by an aunt (whom he believed to be his grandmother) was the root cause of the conflict. At the end he returns to the subject in order to vindicate the father whom he never knew. George Shaw has almost certainly never used the phrase 'tell it like it is', but that is how he has told it.

I freely confess that to me part of the charm of *Sheffielder* is the pleasure of reading names which were familiar forty years ago. Most of the story is set in the Townhead Street Flats – a housing development which has been rebuilt so often that, like those parish churches which were 'improved' with every new architectural style, it became an item of historical interest. I used to stand outside the entrance to those tenements as I waited for the bus that would take me home from what George Shaw describes as 'the secondary school in Leopold Street'. The office in which I worked for the WEA was in Campo Lane – the site of the flats' early extension. During my years as Chairman of the Sheffield Housing Committee, I 'modernized' the Townhead Street Flats at least twice.

As a middle aged man George Shaw visited the philharmonic concerts in the City Hall so often that he must have been in his seat in the gallery on nights when I took my subsidized schoolboy's seat on the platform behind the Hallé Orchestra. I had the better of the bargain, for I looked upon John Barbirolli face to face. George's 'grandmother' is buried in the General Cemetery, itself a memorial to Victorian England. My great grandfather sleeps in a cutler's grave under the brambles and holly which now cover most of the graves. I too have stood on Coles Corner, but while George Shaw watched the Test Match scores which were hung on a board high above the department store, I nervously waited for the girl who had promised to meet me there. Like him I joined the City Library when I was twelve and visited the boating pool in Millhouses Park. George Shaw survived the excursion unscathed. I fell in.

After years of irregular and uncertain employment George Shaw was taken on by Laycocks, a 'supplier of equipment to British and overseas railways companies'. When I was a 'management trainee' at Daniel Doncaster's I applied for a job at Laycocks. They turned me down.

There are so many Sheffield place names, Sheffield characters and

Sheffield prejudices in his book, that George Shaw's chronicles will be read with delight by everybody who knows and loves the city. But it is not intended for Sheffielders alone and it will provide pleasure (and instruction) even for those unfortunates who have never visited the city. E.M. Forster said that *Seven Pillars of Wisdom* was about Lawrence of Arabia's war in the desert in the way that *Moby Dick* is about catching a whale. Literature is about life in general, not the particular. And the tale that George Shaw tells has a universal appeal.

*Sheffielder* is an adventure story. It is not a swashbuckling saga of daring-do. It is an account of a battle for survival. There will be those who say that the author never did anything heroic in his life and that from his rickets-riddled childhood to his late marriage, the only moment of real drama was the blitz of 1940 – a danger that he shared with half a million other Sheffielders.

At 7pm on 12 December, the sirens sounded as I was having a book stamped out in the Central Library. As I walked through the gloom home I was surprised by the zeal of the air-raid wardens and police calling out 'Take shelter.' I soon reached home and after a few minutes it was evident that this was going to be a very different night from those that followed the air-raid warnings that we had had before.

Simple as that account undoubtedly is, it is neither mundane nor prosaic for it gives an insight into one man's feelings. The same can be said about his description of his early working life in a Sheffield forge.

In my earliest days at the job my office, which I shared with the foreman, was a little wooden hutch just inside the shop. . . . As the hammers rose and fell, the whole structure shuddered and trembled.

Not for George Shaw William Cobbett's account of 'gold lit boys dancing in the flame's glare'. But Cobbett was only riding between Sheffield and Leeds and he saw the furnaces from a romantic distance. Shaw was there, sweating it out for a few shillings a week, and hoping for something better.

It would be impossible to pretend that his life has, by the conventional standards of success, been a constant triumph. It has been hard. But he has survived and he has succeeded in writing a book which ought to make readers rejoice at the indomitability of such men as George Shaw.

Roy Hattersley
House of Commons
July 1993

# FIRST LIGHT

What else can I call myself but a Sheffielder? Sheffield was where I was born on 26 February 1912 when the City's prestige as a steel-maker, an armament centre and a producer of cutlery was at its height.

I had no family connection with Sheffield; both my father's and mother's ancestral roots were in the Lincolnshire countryside. My mother came from Deeping St James, not far from Peterborough; my father from Carlton le Moorland, near Lincoln. Only my 'granny' had a Sheffield connection and she, I was later to learn, was not related to me at all.

I was born in a corporation flat in Townhead Street. These particular flats had three levels: a ground-floor flat, a middle flat and a top-floor flat reached by four flights of stone steps, so it was little wonder that within three weeks we moved into a ground-floor flat in Campo Lane. I was among the early babies to be born into that recently created community, in which I was to grow up and live for so many years. Despite the change of address we were still in the same building, for these flats – though usually called Townhead Street Flats – extended over three streets: Townhead Street, Hawley Street and Campo Lane.

I could not walk until I was 5, and my first memories are of using my hands to drag myself about the floor, of the gaslight shining above me and making a bubbling noise, of opening cupboards and getting into them, of being picked up by my mother, and in particular of the 'School Bobby' being at the door in the passage to find out why I hadn't been sent to school. I remember too the stiff black skirts of my granny's sisters at eye level, but I was so close to the ground that I do not remember their faces. In later years my mother told me that people used to say: 'He'll never walk you know. He'll always be like this!'

Before I knew much of the world outside, the interior of our flat gradually unfolded, opening out to my eyes. It was dark during the day, the sun never really penetrated into the living-room because of the flats on the other side (Hawley Street) which reared up and shut out the sun. That is why my childhood memories are of this room at night when the gas was lit – then you could see the shiny black metal of the Yorkshire range with the coal fire glowing and the clank of the heavy oven door opening and shutting. We seemed to have the gaslight on for a lot of the time; it was housed in a glass globe above the table and had a chain by which the light could be regulated. Sometimes the gas mantle, a small white delicate dome, had to be replaced and sometimes there would be a nasty, sickly smell.

Thinking of this early period of my life I have a faint recollection of standing with my hands on a metal ring. I was inside this ring and it moved on wheels; I suppose it must have been a device for teaching me to walk, but all I can remember is my hands on this ring. As I began to stand up after a fashion, one fitting in the flat literally impressed itself on my mind – a large built-in cupboard next to the fireplace. It had three shelves and a huge heavy door that was continually swinging open. Since the bottom was level with my head, I used to collide with it quite often and suffer a deep stunning pain. I can still recall the sensation seventy years later but, thanks to having a thick skull, I suffered no long-term harm.

Along this side of the living-room were the doors of the two bedrooms, and on the far side the wall that ran down to the recess that housed the passage door and what was supposed to be a pantry. The bedrooms were alike in having a window looking into the street, so that they got the sunshine, and each had a fireplace that was never used; any attempt to light a fire resulted in clouds of suffocating smoke filling the flat. One bedroom was larger than the other: the one whose western wall separated us from a similar room in the next flat. Our smaller bedroom was bounded by the wall of the passage and we could hear people on the other side walking upstairs.

Since I was confined to the floor for such a long time, the various items of furniture seemed to me almost alive. In the living-room, the largest room in the flat, there was a big table set on four massive, polished legs which I heard my mother say had been bought from a man who had a big family. The top, when I was able to see it, was plain and unpolished and overhung the sides. There was one large drawer, which squeaked when it was pulled out or pushed shut and frequently seemed to stick.

Under the window that looked into the yard there was a sofa of black horsehair that was shiny and uncomfortable. If you sat on it you seemed to be sliding forward all the time and the curve where one's head was supposed to rest was hard and unfriendly. There was a big dresser with drawers in the middle and a cupboard at either side; it was into these cupboards that I used to crawl to sit among the groceries, with my legs on the floor. Above me on the polished shelf of the dresser was a big glass case containing an enormous stuffed cat. This cat had been the cherished pet of my mother and granny. I was often told how it had come under my chair to die, but I was too young to know what grief was.

There was a set of four heavy, dark-oak chairs in the living-room. One in particular, which stood near the passage door, seemed alive, like an old man waiting to get up. Its thick round legs seemed to be stretched out like a person and there was a presence about its back, which flowed in a broad band over the supports, while its seat, shiny with polish, tilted forward like a human abdomen.

In the bedroom which mother shared with granny there were two large trunks. One was metal and of a dull-green colour; the other, larger one was wooden and creamy brown. Each rested on a large wooden box and since the sides of the boxes were higher at one side than the other there was a space.

At this time, when I was beginning to stand up and walk, I discovered that I could place my tiny hands through the space between trunk and box; at first that was all I could do, but as time passed and my arms grew longer, I was able to reach nearer to the contents of the boxes. There was also a wooden table in the room underneath the window that looked out onto the street. To climb on that table was at 5 an unsatisfied ambition. When I did succeed in scrambling onto it I was to find that its plain top devoid of polish hurt my knees.

The other, bigger bedroom was the one in which I slept on a black, shiny iron bedstead. I recollect lying in bed one day looking at a picture of a big ship which was sinking, with one end up in the air. There were some words on the top of the picture, one of which seemed very long, and I knew it was *Lusitania*. In this room I couldn't get near the window because of a round and rickety bamboo table, and a little dressing table with a mirror and a big washbasin and jug which, I think, had flowers painted on it; but here memory is uncertain, my mental picture of the past flickers.

The greater part of this room was occupied by a bed that had at its head and foot hard lines of black shiny iron struts surmounted at the top by lines of the same shiny black iron. The topmost rung was brass, and on each of the four corners was a fancy brass ornament or knob except that at one of the corners at the bottom of the bed, part of the brasswork had come off and there was no knob, only a length of thread sticking up. This brass bed was occupied during these first five years of my life by someone whom I remember as a voice, as a blur in the bed, a blur that coughed continually and spat and from whose corner of the room came the distinctive sickbed smell, fostered by chamberpots, spittle and stagnant air.

The blur in the bed was my uncle, George William, my mother's elder brother, eight years her senior. He was dying of consumption, slowly wasting away. He was to die five months after my fifth birthday, when he was but 43.

I was named George William in his honour and I think he was fond of me, for on the day the First World War began in 1914 he bought me a toy wheelbarrow on his way home and then took to his bed, never to leave it again. I was told that he came home drunk that day, singing his favourite song 'Won't you come home, Bill Bailey', and struggled up the stairs to the flat we then lived in, holding the wheelbarrow in one hand and shouting 'Prussians are coming'. Of course, it may be that he really intended to say: 'Russians are coming', referring to those phantom warriors with snow on their boots, whose rumoured arrival had raised the spirits of people who felt a sense of bewilderment that our country was involved in a European war, something that had not happened for sixty years, not since the Crimean War. From that day he was too ill to go to work, unable in fact to leave his bed in the room he shared with me.

I was 2½ when the war began, and although I don't remember learning to read, I remember a book which I had to learn my letters. It was a big book of only a few very wide pages, each of which had a number of highly coloured pictures – I for Infantry, A for Artillery, H for Howitzer, and so on. It was certainly very effective and even now I remember many of the letters as they appeared in that book.

Because I always had a good sense of smell, I remember the wartime food-ration books lying on the big table giving out a strong, rank smell, which I think was from the printer's ink. I think they were a yellowish-brown colour. Whatever their colour, it must have been my mother who struggled with them, because granny could neither read nor write. When I was sitting at the big table I could hear my uncle's voice over my shoulder coming from the bedroom.

I remember an episode in which I played a passive part. It was at the time of the great Zeppelin scare; my uncle was very ill and both granny and my mother were in the bedroom attending to him and I was in my mother's bed in the other bedroom. Suddenly I was awake; it was very dark but there was a lot of noise and commotion – somebody was thumping the window glass from outside and shouting something. I have been told it was 'put that light out!' Then someone was in the room lifting me up and I was in the living-room where there was a dim light from a candle. My mother discovered that she had snatched me up legs first but I was told I never made a sound.

The son of my mother's half-sister, Susannah, had joined the Coldstream Guards and was going to France. Before he went he came from Leicester to

Damage following a Zeppelin raid in Crossley Road, September 1916

see his dying uncle. I remember a figure in khaki standing by the bedroom window talking to the blur that was my uncle in the bed. Then next, like a slide on a screen, I am crossing over the railway tracks at the Midland Station perched high up on a khaki shoulder. Now, looking back over seventy years, I feel there must have been an unspoken thought passing between the two men, a thought that they were both going to the same destination; my uncle's consumption, with its coughing, spitting and wasting away was to end his life at 43, and Teddy was soon to die from a sniper's bullet after lingering for a few days in a hospital staffed by nuns. This last detail added to the shock of Teddy's death as far as granny was concerned, for she was prejudiced against Catholics. Those were the days when the newspapers printed long lists of names day after day: of men who had lost their lives, 'killed in action', 'died of wounds', 'missing presumed dead'.

Ted Dickinson, the author's uncle

One of the visitors to my dying uncle was the vicar of St James, the Reverend Dawson Parsons, who once brought him a chicken from his own little flock at the vicarage. Mr Parsons was an Irish Protestant who had served in a mission to navvies and was used to talking to working men. Uncle George William liked him. Mr Parsons was, as people used to say, good with his hands. He painted the church railings, and was a carpenter, wood turner and printer. Noticing me, he asked, 'If you had a wish what would you like to have?'

Clutching at a word I had just heard I said: 'I'd like a submarine!'

'Well, I'll see if I can get you one,' he said.

Of course, the next time he came I asked, 'Have you brought my submarine?'

'No!' he said, 'but I will do!' Sure enough, on the next visit he gave me a wooden ship painted battleship-grey and with two solid wooden funnels rising from the deck. I treasured it for a very long time.

My uncle died in the summer of 1917, but evidently the news did not reach the War Office, for a few months later a paper arrived saying that as a member of the Army Reserve he was being called up for active service. Immediately after his death some men from the council came in a large motor van and took the mattress and all the bedding he had died on for 'stoving'. When the things were brought back, they smelt of smoke and fire, everything was scorched, and when they were washed the sheets and blankets soon developed holes.

I knew little of the war or anything else, for as I have said my world consisted only of those few rooms.

Local historians were puzzled by the name Campo Lane, although some of them derived it from 'camp' which was said to refer to the camp established by the Parliamentarians when they were besieging Sheffield Castle during the Civil War. These flats had been built in 1906 during an

The flats in Townhead Street and Hawley Street, *c.* 1909

early slum-clearance campaign in an area of Sheffield occupied by a desperately poor population that included many Jews and Irish.

The architect had had to design buildings for a site that, like most in Sheffield, was not level. Townhead Street swept down from Church Street in its descent to West Bar. Campo Lane was on top of a slope from which Hawley Street, Silver Street, Paradise Street and North Church Street debouched. The flats were built in two ellipses divided from each other by iron gateways; the Campo Lane, Townhead Street ellipse was on the higher part of the slope and looked down on the flats of the Hawley Street side. Within the two ellipses the flats were built in units of six – a ground-floor flat on each side of a passage with two more flats on each side reached by stone steps.

The gulf between the two sides of the building was so great that a high wall had had to be built in the yard between them, a wall topped by iron spikes. Tucked shamefacedly in a corner of this yard was our coal bunker and lavatory; it was in the lavatory that the gas meter was situated. Not only did it have to be read at intervals, but some sort of adjustment involving water had to be made when the gas light dipped and bobbled. Stone steps led up from the yard to the glass-panelled door of our short narrow kitchen, which had a stone sink and a brick-built 'copper' intended for the boiling of clothes in water heated by a small fireplace.

I could gaze into this yard and into the street from the windows of the flat, which had so far been the limits of my world, but not until I was past 5 did the outside begin to take shape and meaning.

My mother had taken me in her arms to the passage door to show me to the School Attendance Officer to prove the truth of what she had told him. My weak spine and rickets had confined me and were to stop me starting school until I was 8 years old.

First I learned about the flats around us, individual buildings, the known world extending all the time. Now as I look back it seems like the raising of the curtains in a theatre, curtain after curtain rising, the thick outer curtain, the fire curtain, and then thinner and thinner films of drapery as the eye sees farther and farther back and the light strengthens.

But before I describe my district and the face of Sheffield as it was revealed to me, there are family matters relating to those living at 92 Campo Lane when I was an infant, matters that affected my own life then and for long afterwards. For this I must begin another chapter.

# CHAPTER TWO

# GRANNY'S STORY

In the flat in my childhood my mother was always at hand to comfort me when I was in pain, but she was not the most dominant spirit in the household. That was the old lady whom I then believed to be what I called her, my granny; she had a strong will and a fiery temper. As I remember her, she was a thinnish, rather bony woman with a sharp tongue, prepared to stick up for what she thought was right against anybody. Her hair was grey or white, there was not much of it, and when she went out it was covered by a black bonnet tied under the chin. On special occasions this was replaced by a black and red one normally kept in a round hatbox. She was a very formidable person, and although she loved both my mother and me I am sure that she broke up my mother's marriage and deprived me of a father. She was the only one of the four of us living at 92 Campo Lane who had an ancestral connection with Sheffield.

She was a widow and her name was Mrs Knight, but she had been born in Allen Street, Sheffield, in 1847 as Lucy Ann Ashton, the eldest of the five children of John Ashton, who later became the landlord of the Wellington Inn on Penistone Road. This inn must have had a sign because granny said that it had a picture of 'the hero on his horse'. Only one of the five Ashton children was a boy, Frederick. He and a sister called Emily Eliza died while the family were living at the Wellington Inn. Granny was very fond of her brother Frederick and there was one little ornament in our flat that was very dear to her — a pottery figure of a ram which had been her brother's favourite toy. I still have it, but during the passage of time it has been chipped on one side. At one time I also had some large, clumsy-looking knives and forks which were stamped with the words: 'John Ashton. Wellington Inn'. These vanished years ago. The Wellington was an unlucky home for the Ashtons; the two children who died there were followed by their father in 1858.

The widow had a sister who was married to a farmer named Hall whose farm was near the village of Bradfield in the Loxley valley to the north-west of Sheffield and it was there that the widow Ashton went to live, taking Lucy Ann and her two younger sisters, Sarah Elizabeth and Hetty.

Only three years later, in 1861, the sisters became orphans when their mother died. Lucy Ann regarded herself as the champion and protector of her younger sisters and she must have been a difficult and unruly child to bring up. Once, she recalled, after a heated argument she was taken upstairs and locked in an empty room; at this time remember the only illumination would have been candles and oil lamps. It was night and at first everything was pitch-black. Then, as her eyes became adjusted to the dark, she saw a white figure in a corner of the room. She was always superstitious and now her scalp tingled, her hair seemed about to stand on end and she broke into a cold sweat. At first she was too terrified to make a sound but then she screamed and screamed until her aunt came and unlocked the door. By candlelight she could then see that the ghost in the corner was one of her uncle's white shirts hanging on a clothes horse.

Lucy Ann was still living at the farm in March 1864 when a dam burst in the valley below, sending a wall of water that spread death and destruction along the course of the Loxley to Sheffield. It made a great impression on her mind and I noticed as I grew up that she and many old people used it as a benchmark, saying 'before the Flood' or 'since the Flood'. It is a curious circumstance that most of the events in Sheffield's history that stand out, that brought Sheffield into the news, have been misfortunes such as the cholera epidemic, the Flood, the trade union outrages, the Blitz of 1940 and, most recently, the Hillsborough football disaster.

I imagine that the Hall's uncle and aunt felt they had done their duty by the orphans in giving them food and shelter, so as soon as possible they were packed off to 'service' and not only that but they lost touch with one another. In the case of Lucy Ann, not only was she without parents and had lost sight of her sisters but she suffered from a grievous handicap that followed her all the days of her life – she could not read or write. Her sister, Sarah Elizabeth, also had a rebellious disposition, which caused her uncle and aunt to place her in a Girls' Charity School on Campo Lane where she was frequently beaten for what was called 'her naughtiness'. Years passed and the girls were almost adults when my granny Lucy Ann discovered her sister Sarah Elizabeth working as a servant to a couple of old maids who kept a tea shop in Angel Street. She also made contact with her other sister, Hetty, but what had happened to Hetty in the intervening years I do not know.

At this time, the last quarter of the nineteenth century, Sheffield was rapidly expanding and was a magnet for many people from rural

George Knight who died in 1876

Lincolnshire, where the only work was on the land, in domestic service and on the railway. It was a Lincolnshire immigrant, George Knight, that Lucy Ann Ashton married. George Knight was said to have worked in some of the big works, but as he was also said to have worked on the extensions for Cockaynes shop he may have been a building worker like his brother-in-law, Dennis Kusick, who was a bricklayer at the time he married granny's sister, Sarah Elizabeth. How long George Knight stayed in Sheffield after marrying Lucy Ann I do not know, but for some reason he wanted to return to Lincolnshire.

In the south of Lincolnshire there is a group of villages called the Deepings: Market Deeping, Deeping St James, Deeping St Nicholas, West Deeping and Deeping Gate. When George Knight returned to the

Deepings he got a job granny described as 'cleaning the river', the river in question being the Welland. Granny was happy at Deeping; she was passionately fond of dancing and walked to every dance in the district. After dancing to the early hours of the morning she would stride home shoes in hand, for her feet were too sore after hours of dancing to bear the constraint of shoes.

The people of the village had their own way of dealing with those who offended against the moral code – wife-beaters, adulterers and others. As a child I was told of occasions when a crowd of villagers equipped with saucepans, kettles, plates and anything that would make a noise would assemble and march to the cottage of some offender, evil-liver or petty thief and would bang, clatter and rattle their collection of domestic hardware, chanting: 'Ran Tan Tan! He's a very bad man!'

The Knights lived in Deeping St James, where George Knight's sister, my grandmother Hester Elizabeth, was married to my grandfather William Green. William Green had already buried one wife, Betsy Teat, by whom he had a daughter, Susannah. By his second wife he had four sons, Jim, Tom, George William and Edward (Ted). Then, on 5 July 1882, my mother was born. She was christened Lucy Mary, but her mother died about three weeks afterwards and was buried in the village of Glinton where she had been married in 1873.

Following the death of his second wife, my grandfather William Green must have been relieved when his sister-in-law Lucy Ann took over the care of his young family. He soon seems to have overcome his sorrow at the death of his wife, for by 1884 he had remarried. His new bride was a widow with three children, and he later became the father of another daughter, Nell.

George Knight and Lucy Ann had no children of their own but what George thought of Lucy taking charge of his sister's five young children is not known. Whatever his job of 'cleaning the river' entailed, it did not do his health any good for in a few years he was dead. It was not only foul weather and water he had to contend with. Granny told us how dangerous it was in the fogs of winter, when it was easy to step off the path into the river and be carried away with no one to hear a cry for help or, if they heard, to do anything in time. George died in 1890 at the age of 38 and possibly he had been ailing for a long time. My mother's strongest memory of her childhood at Deeping St James was of a time when the Welland burst its banks and the water poured into the Knights' cottage. Lucy Ann snatched up my mother and two of her brothers, all infants, and dropped them into the dolly tub she used for washing the laundry. The children floated about the flooded kitchen in this tub as if it was a miniature Ark.

Mother (left) and Granny, *c.* 1895

It seems as if the arrangement by which Lucy Ann mothered her sister-in-law's children lasted for some ten years. Then in 1893 the pattern of life changed again for all of them. The eldest boy, George William (who in my childhood lived and died with us in the flat), was by this time 19 years of age. He fell passionately in love with a girl in the village who eventually rejected him. In those days many a lad, victim of unrequited love, would cry 'I'll go for a sodger', for it was one of the few avenues of escape from life in the village and there seemed something romantic in the idea of taking the Queen's shilling, of showing how deeply the girl had wounded her lover. The official record shows that George William joined the Royal Regiment of Artillery on 13 November 1893 at Stamford. But according to my mother he had made an earlier attempt to join the Tenth Foot, the Lincolnshire Regiment also known as 'The Dirty Tenth'; why he failed to enlist in the infantry is a mystery. In October 1894, now in the Royal Garrison Artillery, he was sent to India where he spent the next nine years, most of the time at Roorkee. It must have been a very boring and monotonous life from which beer offered the only escape; did he regret

School group at Market Deeping, Lincolnshire, 1890. Mother is in the second row from the front, fifth from the left

joining the colours and spending his youth in the heat of India? There is one curious item in his 'Account Book and Pocket Ledger' 0544 in which a soldier's savings (if any) were recorded. From the time of his enlistment, month after month passes with not one penny in his savings account. Then in September 1897 a balance of £26 7s 10d appears, which by October 1897 had shrunk to £23 11s 9d. The next month the figure was nil, and so it remained for the rest of his service. Where did the money come from and what happened to it? My theory is that he won it gambling and then 'blued it' on his comrades or perhaps sent some home.

George William's younger brothers had also reached the age when they could work for a living. Jim and Ted went to Leicester, where their half-sister Susannah lived, William Green's daughter by his first wife. She had a warm spot in her heart for her half-brothers and first Jim and then Ted went to Leicester to live with her and her husband, who was a farm worker. Jim got a job with the city's electricity department and Ted became a leather worker, making saddles and harness for the horses not yet challenged by the automobile. Ted was the dandy of the family, said my mother, always very

Sue Melborn, girlfriend of
George William Green

particular about his shoes and shirts and general apparel, spending a lot of
time on his appearance. Tom, alone of the children of Hester Elizabeth and
William Green, stayed in the village of Deeping St James and was to spend
his life in the service of the railway.

By this time my mother was 12 years old. The only other memory she
passed on to me of her childhood in Deeping St James was of paying a
penny a week for the privilege of going to school.

With the remarriage of George Knight's brother-in-law, William Green,
in 1884, the death of George Knight in 1890, and lastly the ability of
George Knight's nephews the four Green boys to look after themselves,
there was by 1894 nothing to hold the Sheffield-born widow Lucy Ann
Knight in Deeping St James. She was regarded by the young Greens as their
mother, and had she remained this might have later led to a conflict of
loyalties. Now with my mother, her adopted daughter who worshipped her,
she left the Deepings for Sheffield.

CHAPTER THREE

# A LOST FATHER

When the two Lucys arrived in Sheffield, it was a city of 338,000 inhabitants and still expanding. The pall of smoke that hung over it was a source of pride to its citizens – 'Where there's muck there's money.'

Lucy Ann Knight was the aunt by marriage of her adopted daughter, Lucy Mary Green, who had known no other mother. At first they lived at School Lane, Crookes, with Lucy Ann's sister Hetty, of whom I know very little. After a few weeks they moved to No. 3, Railway Cottages, Rock Street, in the district called Pye Bank near to Pitsmoor. These cottages were built on top of a railway tunnel and when an express train bustled through beneath the cottages the vibrations set up made the cups and saucers dance about on the shelves and everything shake.

In one of the other cottages in the row lived a young woman called Sally, who was a seamstress by trade and worked in the sewing room of Coles department store. In those days Sally dressed very smartly and took great pride in her appearance. The way to the street from the cottage in which she lived led past the small garden belonging to the cottage where the two Lucys had their home. In 1894 ladies wore long dresses sweeping the floor and by and by Sally came to Lucy Ann with a grievance and a request.

'Your flowers disarrange my skirt!' she said. 'Kindly remove them!'

'That I shall not,' was the reply. 'I like flowers.'

Nothing more was said, but early next morning Sally came into the garden with a pair of scissors and cut off the heads of all the flowers. Sally was triumphant, Lucy Ann and my mother were indignant and it was years before the breach was healed and they spoke to one another again. When they did meet much later, Sally had become a member of a group within the Plymouth Brethren who led lives of extreme piety and self-denial in which pleasure was regarded as an evil, something liable to promote the lusts of the flesh.

Lucy Ann Knight earned her living by taking in washing and going out

Pye Bank, *c.* 1895, where mother and granny lived when they first moved to Sheffield. The crosses indicate houses to be demolished

Rock Street, Pye Bank, *c.* 1895

cleaning – charring for women able to afford to pay for help with the rougher household tasks. Soon after the arrival of the two Lucys in Sheffield there was a terrible winter when everything was frozen up and there was a great shortage of work. My mother and Lucy Ann were short of money to buy food and fuel and nearly starved to death. It was experiences like these, shared together, that bound my mother to her aunt.

Thanks to being able to read and write my mother was a great help to the older woman, who was very suspicious of being deceived and swindled by those who were literate, particularly lawyers. It seems that in connection with a will she had been called to a lawyer's office and asked to make her mark on a document which she said signed away her right to a lot of money; she had been given a very small sum which she was sure was totally unjust.

In 1898, when my mother was 16, the two women moved to a block of offices in Meetinghouse Lane in what was called the Legal Quarter of Sheffield, when Lucy Ann was appointed as a living-in caretaker. The area has not changed much since 1898, it is still the Legal Quarter although now accountants and building societies have muscled in on the lawyers.

At the other side of the block of offices was Figtree Lane, a narrow cobbled lane where halfway down behind iron gates was a large cobbled courtyard. Also quite close to it in the Lane was a building which had once been Sheffield's first women's hospital. All this Legal Quarter – Bank Street, Church Street, North Church Street, Hartshead – was a district where Charles Dickens would have been at home for it was not until the end of the Second World War that most offices underwent a modest modernization. The living quarters where the two Lucys were to live for the next eleven years were at the top of the building, overlooking the cobbled courtyard just mentioned.

The firm which occupied this building was a long-established, highly respected family firm of lawyers – respected not only for their legal ability but because by this time they were a family of country gentry living in a Georgian house to the north-west of Sheffield. The old gentleman who was head of the family and the firm was regarded with affection and respect by his staff, including the two females in the flat at the top of the building. No one felt affection or respect for the eldest son, the future head of the family. He was a cold, snobbish, fishlike creature. 'Fishlike' is a good description, for to call him 'stony' might have suggested that like stone he could absorb warmth. My mother and Lucy Ann hated to meet him on the stairs or in the corridors, for he never spoke or acknowledged their existence. He simply walked past them in silence and if he was unable to avoid looking at them would stare as if they were not there and did not exist.

No one could understand how he had become engaged to the daughter

Hicks Lane in 1900

of an earl, a girl who seemed to have all the human qualities her future husband lacked. Sometimes she visited him at his place of work, arriving either in a horse-drawn carriage emblazoned with the family crest or riding on a beautiful horse. My mother always remembered the first time she had to take refreshments into the private office where the distinguished visitor was waiting until her fiancé was able to break away from work. With trembling hands my mother took the silver tray into the Presence. In this period at the end of the century the aristocracy was a world apart. Their political power had faded, but socially they still occupied the highest place in the land, just below the Royal Family in the eyes of those at the bottom of the social ladder. My mother was greatly impressed by the noble lady's demeanour, the way she put the little waitress at ease, spoke to her as one girl to another and seemed genuinely interested in details of her family background. My mother retreated, no longer nervous and fearful, but admiring and making comparisons in her mind with the boorish prospective husband of this paragon.

Mother in 1901 at the age of 19 years

During the years spent in the flat at the top of the lawyers' offices, my mother attended the Parish Church Mission at the Wolstenholme Hall in Queen Street. This was before the parish church of Sheffield was elevated to cathedral status when the new bishopric of Sheffield was created. My mother was not a really pious person but she enjoyed attending the Mission at the Wolstenholme Hall and always spoke warmly of Archdeacon Blakeney, who played a prominent part in the activities there. She won at least two prizes when she attended the Mission. One I still have is *The Life of General Gordon* by Demetrious C. Boulger, which was presented to her on 4 January 1903. The other volume, which has been lost, was an account of popular Chinese superstitions written by a Christian missionary in a very hostile spirit; it also contained an account of various Chinese tortures. I doubt if she read a word of either book. The odd thing is that both books had her name inscribed as Lucy Knight, when she was really Lucy Green; already other people thought Lucy Ann Knight was her mother.

Mother's brother, George William, returned from India in 1902 and the rest of his service was spent in the United Kingdom. He was discharged from the army at Seaforth near Liverpool on 10 November 1905. He then came to Sheffield and joined his sister and aunt in the caretaker's quarters in Meetinghouse Lane; it must have been crowded in the flat at the top of the office building but Deeping, his childhood home, held the memories of the unhappy love affair. The army had taught him only two things: to drive horses and to drink. He got a job driving a horse and dray through the city for one of the railway companies; this was a job in which he was exposed year in and year out to the worst the English climate could do and gradually constant exposure to the wet undermined his health. Drink perhaps accelerated the consumption which was to kill him; unlike some drinkers he was never quarrelsome or nasty-tempered or lost command of his wits. He told them that in Liverpool at the end of his army service: 'In an Orange pub I was Orange and in an Irish pub I was Catholic.'

At about this time, 1905, the Sheffield Corporation was building the block of flats which were to be known as Townhead Street Flats. They were an early piece of slum clearance, as they replaced an unsavoury district called The Crofts where it is known that a sizeable proportion of the inhabitants were Jews and Irish. Lucy Ann Knight set her heart on getting one of these flats as soon as they were completed. Whatever the reason, it was not until 1908 that she, George William and my mother left Meetinghouse Lane for the flats.

Apart from the move to the flats there was another development. On the evidence of her photographs my mother was then a handsome, fresh-faced young woman with an open, innocent expression. She must have attracted admirers before my father but she never spoke of them. My father, William Shaw, was another emigrant from Lincolnshire; he originated from Eagle, a tiny village about six miles south-west of Lincoln containing a church, a pub and nothing much else. His father was a farm labourer, as was his father before him. William was a member of a large family, all of whom were distinguished by black hair and a gypsy appearance said to have been brought into the family by a Spanish lady. My mother, Lucy Mary, liked him and she met his family to mutual approval. She and his youngest sister struck up a friendship which lasted until Frances emigrated to Canada.

Mother began to be independent of Lucy Knight; in 1908 she went with

Mother and father before their marriage, *c.* 1909

William Shaw on a trip to the Franco-British Exhibition in London. Eventually in 1909 the couple were married at All Saints church in the Ellesmere district of the city. Trouble seems to have begun almost at once. William wanted to provide a home. He wanted his wife to leave the flat in Townhead Street to which she had moved with her aunt. There is no doubt that Lucy Knight feared my mother's departure. Who would read the letters and official forms that came for her? Who would tell her what was in the newspapers? Who would read inscriptions in shops, street names and a hundred other things? She clung desperately to her niece. I can imagine that she must have appealed to my mother's sense of loyalty, reminded her of how she had looked after her from being a helpless baby three weeks old. No doubt Lucy Knight made much of such faults of my father's as appeared to come to light, to poison my mother's love for him. The result was that my mother forgot the words in the marriage service about 'forsaking all others' for she allowed herself to be convinced that her true loyalty was to the woman who had brought her up.

My mother was a very stubborn woman, a quality I am said to have inherited, and I am sure in what must have been many painful arguments her attitude, apparently so unreasonable, must have hardened under argument and criticism to conviction that she should stick to Lucy Knight. The final break came two or three weeks after I was born and so it was that I never knew my father and I only came to know his side of the family after he was dead, and long after they had left Eagle for Carlton-le-Moorland, another village about seven miles south of Lincoln.

CHAPTER FOUR

# DISCOVERIES

Now I reach the point in my story where I was at last able to stand up unaided on my legs and look at the world around me – the world I could see from the windows of our ground-floor flat. The first view that I recall is the yard behind the flats from the living-room window. I have no idea of the date but I am sure it must have been winter and a Sunday, for it was very quiet, grey and cold and I feel that it was early in the morning.

I could not see far – my vision was limited by the flats at the other side of the yard, and much nearer to me was a stone wall which had a fence of black metal spikes joined together at top and bottom to make them continuous. Of course, although I saw this and other things, it took a long time to know what they were. Behind the metal frame, for instance, there was a yawning gap to the bottom of the other side of the yard; in days to come I was to know boys who for a dare would walk along behind the fence from one end to the other, passing the point opposite our flat where, if they had slipped, they would have fallen 20 feet to the stone floor of the yard. Beyond the metal fence rose the shapes of the flats in Hawley Street – great brick structures, with oblong verandahs on each side of flights of stairs. On that first morning and immediately afterwards before I had come to know what the different shapes signified, I was puzzled by people appearing and disappearing, going up and down the stairs and vanishing, and other people appearing on the balconies.

Now that I could walk about instead of crawling on the floor the world about me grew bigger. Every time I woke up to a new day there was a fresh sight, sound or experience to mentally digest. Now I understood that as far as I could see the flats extended in lines until, far away it seemed, the intervening wall ended and the yard continued, and after a time I could see a big metal gate that marked the end of the world. This was looking down the slope. When I turned round, there too the two lines of flats ended in a wall and a metal gate. After a while it dawned on me that all the flats were arranged in the same way, with three on one side of the passage and three on the other.

Also I began to be aware of sounds. The sound of people going up and down the steps, people walking about in the floor above us, the sound of coal fires being poked and mended all round us, sacks of coal being unloaded in coal bunkers and then sounds from the street outside. In time I was aware of the other people who lived in our passage. As I came to realize in later life, these were the people who could make life tolerable or hellish.

Lucy Ann Knight I now knew as granny and she used to say that we lived in the best passage in the flats. All the tenants were nice people and though the bottom flat where we lived, being nearer the outside dust and muck, was dirtier than the others, it was more convenient not to have to lug parcels and shopping up and down stairs and from outside. Looking through the window, we could even tell the time from the Town Hall clock.

Sheffield Town Hall, c. 1900

I didn't notice much from the front windows for quite a time – not until I found a way of hauling myself onto the plain wooden table that stood under the bedroom window next to the passage entrance. Peering through the window I could look out onto a road junction. Here Campo Lane came from my left and ended at Townhead Street, which ran downhill to my right and in front went up a steep rise to where the tramlines ran across the top. They went from Church Street on the left to West Street on the right. At the top of the hill I could see the beginning of another street, Leopold Street, and closing the view there, the Town Hall tower surmounted by the figure of Vulcan, the Smith of the Gods. That tower has something of the appearance of a giant grandfather clock, a thought that did not occur to me until I was much older. I might say that even with the aid of spectacles I was never able to tell the time from it, as many people in the flats could.

Two buildings, one on the corner of Campo Lane and the other at the right-hand side of the road facing, engaged my attention at once.

On the left was the pub, the Golden Ball, with one entrance at the junction of the two streets, then a length of facade, then four stone steps leading to the tap room; beyond the steps the building ended in a blank wall. The other side of the Golden Ball, in Townhead Street, had a door through which you could reach the Best Room, which would I suppose today be called the Lounge. Next door on Townhead Street was a small office building and then the black iron railings with a gate in the middle behind which was the graveyard leading to the church of St James.

One of the first sights that met my eyes when I looked from my vantage point on the table was the roadway black with people. They were standing about watching a fight between two men. The crowd moved backwards and forwards as the combatants swayed to and fro. Finally one man fell on the ground and the other jumped on him and banged his head on the roadway. That is all I remember. Things seemed to erupt suddenly into violence and finish as suddenly. To a child it was all bewildering.

About the same time, or so it seemed, there was another fight, between two women; this time I was in the crowd surrounding them. This seemed much more bewildering, because there was so much shouting going on. Some people were encouraging the fighters and others trying to pass by them, with momentary lulls broken by one or other of the two antagonists flying at her opponent, trying to scratch her face or pull her hair out.

If I turned my gaze to the right through the window I could see a large building, an orange-coloured building, that straggled up that side of Townhead Street round the corner into Trippet Lane. This had, I think, four storeys, maybe five, and it was demolished in about 1970. When I was looking through my window it was occupied by a large garage belonging to a firm called The Yorkshire Motor Co. What fascinated me about it was that all the red vans of the Royal Mail were based there and used to be parked in the street. Once a mischievous boy from farther down the street climbed into a van and set it going, but although this caused a sensation among the flat dwellers little damage or harm was done, either to the van or the boy. The garage was of particular interest to me because the father of Tommy, who lived across the passage from us, worked for a time in the workshop there. He was a very skilful mechanic and a man able to turn his hand to anything. This perhaps explains why he didn't get called up for the army; he was too useful. He had the same name as his son and so he was called Old Tom; his boy was always known as Young Tom.

I've already mentioned the evil-smelling ration books but apart from our rations we sometimes used to get a treat from my mother's half-sister, Susannah. Her husband was the bailiff or farm manager at a sewage farm owned by Leicester Corporation. Every now and then a wooden box would arrive, nailed securely together, and when it was opened there would be cake, cheese, egg custard and eggs. On one occasion a railway drayman came to the passage door of our flat and handed over just such a box and departed. I stood expectantly, peering over the edge of the big table at the box. Why were granny and mother taking such a time to open it? Then came a knock at the door and it was the drayman again. Very sorry but he'd made a mistake! The box was for a flat with the same number, 92, in the next street. So off went the box and I, who had been eagerly speculating on what was inside, was given the first of many lessons on not to count on anything.

The world was gradually expanding around me, as if curtains were being raised disclosing buildings farther and farther away. In later years when I passed the Cutlers Hall on Church Street I would be reminded of going to a Christmas Party there organized by the Sunshine Society for poor and crippled children, at about the time when I had just begun to walk. There was a lot of noise and we sat at tables with white tablecloths, and at the top of the table was a large copper tea urn. We were given an apple and an orange each as we went downstairs to Church Street when it was all over.

I discovered that beyond the Golden Ball there were slummy stone houses whose stonework had gone black with smoke, and shops. Next to the houses was a yard belonging to our local coal merchant and then a shop selling groceries, then a lodging house belonging to the coal merchant's wife, then there was a little shop at the corner of Vicar Lane – this sold newspapers. Most of Campo Lane was still unknown territory to me and it was a long time before I was aware that there was the other block of flats nearby, Hawley Street Flats – not as good as ours, everyone said.

Recruting for the First World War at Bramall Lane football ground, 1914

New recruits for the First World War outside Cole Brothers Ltd, 1914

# DISCOVERIES

While the knowledge of this was still in the future, I remember being brought out of our passage and looking along Campo Lane. It was a dark misty night, the gaslight seemed to create islands of orange-coloured mist and there as I looked I could see some pairs of trouser legs just disappearing from sight. There was no noise, no traffic, just a sinister feeling. At that time, I heard people say, there was another pub, a little one, at the same side as the Golden Ball, on the other side of Vicar Lane, where long afterwards Silverstones were to erect their cabinet maker's emporium.

I think it must have been about the time when I acquired my window on the world that something happened at the Golden Ball. It was winter and there was snow on the ground. A few feet from our passage the yard sloped steeply downwards and the children of the area found it to be an ideal sledging course. The boy from the pub had a better sledge than most of the other children but something went wrong as he careered down the slope and he was thrown into a wall, with fatal consequences.

It may have been that winter that I went to another party, smaller than the one in the Cutlers Hall. I think it was Christmas again, for it was cold and dark outside the flats. A lady collected me from our flat and I think she had another boy with her. We got on a tram at the top of the street and seemed to make a long journey to a strange part of the city where there were big houses with gardens in front. We got off the tram and entered what seemed a very luxurious house where there was a big table set for tea. There were some grown-ups and what seemed like a lot of children, some of whom seemed to live there. After consuming the good things on the table, we played games – musical chairs, hide-and-seek, and others – and then it was all over and we went home. It was such a wonderful experience, I couldn't believe that it wouldn't happen again, and for years afterwards I tried to find the house where this wonderful party had been held but never did.

There were other sights to watch from my window. Between the flats and the Golden Ball was an area of level ground – well, ground that was as level as you will find anywhere in hilly Sheffield. Here those men with horse-drawn vehicles would stop to rest their animals before they tackled the steep hill to Leopold Street. There were the big carts used for transporting loose coal and other loose and bulky substances, railway drays carrying parcels, flat drays with bars of steel, Waterhouse's flat carts with salt, milk floats, Rington's tea vans, and now and again funeral hearses and carriages. I well remember the horses standing with steam rising from their bodies and then the drivers, when they had decided to charge up the hill, gathering the reins in one hand and leading the horse at a run, shouting encouragement as they struggled up towards the tramlines. If going up the hill with a dray horse was arduous, perhaps even worse was coming down with the brake on and a plate under the back wheel to slow progress.

There was another sight which impressed itself on me in those days when I saw the world around me through the bedroom window. Behind the Golden Ball, the grey-black mass of St James peeped over the pub roof. Its tower was like a number of stone cubes surmounted by a little dome like a cap, held up by a number of round pillars — how many I can't remember. Now that Uncle George William was dead I slept in the bedroom next to the passage, the room whose window afforded me a glimpse of the world outside. Here every Sunday morning I would hear the solitary bell of St James calling the faithful to the service. It had an unmistakable sound as if there was a crack in it somewhere; perhaps it depended on the ringer, for sometimes it had an urgent sound. We never went, because my mother never had any money to spare for the collection and was too proud to go and fail to contribute.

Near the end of the war in 1918 I was able to walk quite well — in fact my mother and granny found my ceaseless pacing up and down the flat an irritation but our doctor said: 'Leave him alone! Let him walk as much as he likes.' He had always maintained that I would be able to walk and even though our neighbours used to say that I was doomed to crawl about the floor like a spider, his view prevailed. The arrival of the doctor was a matter of great consequence in those days. For one thing he would arrive in a car. Then he would descend and march decisively down the passage, rap on the door opening it at the same time, and enter exuding an aroma of bath salts or scent, clad immaculately in a dark suit and spotless white shirt with a high collar.

One sign of the war was the number of wounded soldiers in sky-blue uniforms in the streets, some of them able to walk about albeit with arms in slings, sometimes with only one arm, others with crutches and some of them with missing legs; other poor fellows in wheelchairs or great big things like coffins on wheels in which only their faces could be seen as they were wheeled about. There were always people collecting for war charities. Once there were nurses and ambulance drivers from the Western Front with motor ambulances that were all tatters from shellfire. I remember one of them being in Leopold Street with the nurses rattling collecting tins. Another time when people stood around rattling collecting boxes it was called 'Feed the Guns' and I was taken on my newly nimble legs to Barker's Pool, that street where early and primitive Sheffield had obtained its water supply, to see a great assembly of artillery. There were guns and limbers, brass and steel gleaming and shining. They seemed so big, yet in a way they just seemed bigger versions of the toys I and my friend Tommy played with

Neighbours Mr and Mrs Jennings outside the flats, *c.* 1920. George is the small boy in the doorway

on his tabletop. Somehow they didn't seem the same weapons that were being used at the Front.

Like many children I listened to the conversation of grown-ups without understanding what was said, but sensing approval and disapproval from the tone of voice. Thus, listening to the gossip of our neighbours, I formed the opinion that women munition workers were a flighty lot and I couldn't understand what some women on the flats could have done to cause their husbands to be angry. 'When he comes back,' it was said, 'there'll be hell to play.'

Even the biggest war has to have an end. I recall the flags being put out, more people than usual in the streets, and on the Moor the verandah of a pub called the Pump being beautifully decorated with flowers and flags. I can't remember anyone being very gay and joyful even though this must have been the Armistice.

Tommy, who lived in the other ground-floor flat across our passage, went to Bow Street school, the school I should have gone to, and he and some other children came back from school one day dressed in what was supposed to be armour — silver armour, with silver shields and swords made of cardboard and wood. They were supposed to be crusaders.

Below the Yorkshire Motors garage there was a workshop, and below that a flight of steps led up a steep slope to Trippet Lane; this slope was called Little Hill and soon after the war it was taken over as a clubhouse for the newly formed British Legion. This occasioned events I particularly enjoyed watching. Once a dignitary came to open the new club. The street was filled with people from wall to wall, side to side, as the dignitary came, lolling back in a limousine. It made very slow progress through the crowd, who seemed to engulf it. Best of all, after the club was opened there would be great processions of ex-servicemen marching down the hill from Leopold Street, and just outside my window a military band would play music, sad, noble, nostalgic music, 'Old Comrades', 'The Passing of the Regiments', etc. I think all this must have been for Armistice Day in the days when people still thought the Great War would be the last of its kind.

In my next memory I am outside in the yard with some other children. We are all standing by the wall with its metal fencing; on each side of the fence the wall is smooth and runs level to my right until it ends, but on the left the wall runs down a slope until it comes to an end a very long way off. We have got bricks, bright red bricks, and we push them up and down the wall, in fact we run with them because we are railway engines and we shout 'Choo! Choo!' as we go along. We have accidents on the railway, one engine crashes into another, and I can still feel the hot pain and smart when my hand is trapped between two bricks.

I recall a frightening experience that befell me and some of my fellow train drivers. We were kneeling down on the stone paving of the yard and some of us had pieces of stick with which we were scraping away at the earth where one paving stone barely met another. Suddenly out of the earth emerged a brown length of round material that oozed out onto the surface of the yard. It was of course a worm. Everyone drew back in fear and somebody said, 'It's a snake!' and then we train drivers grabbed a piece of stone or brick and set to beating the thing as long as it moved until it was pulp.

One of our most popular games was Hide-and-seek, and you can be sure there was no shortage of hiding places in all the passages and stairways and in the recesses where the coal bunkers and lavatories were housed. If one of the hiders was discovered he would run away and if you caught him or her up, they would turn round, put their hands up and cry 'Kamerad', a word we had got from the soldiers on leave or maybe the papers.

I remember a story that people laughed about, but I'm not sure whether it was during the war or just after. This concerned a lady in one of the middle flats. She was the mistress of a married man who used to visit her frequently. One day the husband paid a visit to his lady love unaware that his wife, long suspicious, had tracked him to the flats. The wife waited for a while, hoping to catch the lovers *in flagrante delicto*, then hurried up the stairs and tried to open the door – it was locked. She called out: 'I know you're in there! Let me in!' and hammered furiously on the door.

The lady of the house put on a performance worthy of a great comedy actress, behaving as if awakened from a deep sleep and crying: 'Who is it? What do you want? Wait a minute while I find the key!' While she was thus fighting a rearguard action, the erring husband crept onto the verandah, climbed over the spiked railings at the end and slid down the pillar that held the verandahs up. Meanwhile the wife, having at length been admitted, could only scream in baffled fury to find her quarry gone.

# CHAPTER FIVE

# NEIGHBOURS

Now I want to describe the people who lived in our passage, and here too my realization of who lived on top and around us was a gradual process. The passage was, and for that matter still is, the unit in the Townhead Street flats. My mother and my granny were never tired of blessing their good fortune at having such virtuous neighbours in ours.

As I have said, the ground-floor flat on the other side of our passage was occupied by Young Tom and his father Old Tom and Grace, Young Tom's mother. Grace was a very gentle, refined woman who was devoted to her son. There was some friction between husband and wife because Old Tom liked his drink and Grace objected to him coming home drunk. He was what working-class people call 'genuine' – he earned good money but was generous with it and was always ready to help anyone who needed help, getting up in the night to assist the sick and dying, a man people would rely on, the sort of man happier in his working clothes than dressed up. One thing Tom and Grace shared together was pride in and devotion to their brilliant son. Young Tom was more than two years older than me so that though we played together we were not really friends. It was a case of the leader and the led. Even as a young boy he was a very good draughtsman; when we and other children played with him he was the one with ideas of what to do. I was to lose sight of him when I was about 13 years old and didn't meet him again until after the Second World War, when his life was to come to an untimely end.

Time now to go up the steps to the next floor. The flat above us, No. 96, was occupied by two maiden ladies who were dressmakers. Their treadle sewing machine made a thumping noise hour after hour but I hardly noticed it, for I had heard the noise ever since I had been aware of my surroundings.

At the other flat on that level, the one above Young Tommy's, which was No. 94, there was a girl called Mary who was Tommy's age. The two grown-ups who lived in the flat with her seemed very, very old to me. The husband was a little bent man with one shoulder lower than the other, a lot of white hair and spectacles. He was always dressed in a sober black suit; had I been older I should have probably thought he was a professor but in fact he was a piano tuner at Wilson Pecks, the famous and old-established music shop on Leopold Street. Strangely enough I can't remember his wife, except that she was a short, plump woman. Somehow I never wondered why Mary should be so young and yet live with people so old. They were of course her grandparents and if they looked worried and sad it was because of a family tragedy. Their only daughter, a smart, pretty girl, had worked in an office where she attracted the attention of a married man who never ceased to pursue her until he had succeeded in seducing her. When she became pregnant, her lover dropped her and she was left to bear the child on her own. It is a commonplace story but of course to people of her parents' generation it was a terrible disgrace. When she died in childbirth they were left with a continuing reminder of their dead girl as they strove to bring up their granddaughter.

In the flat above them lived Sally, the lady who when granny and my mother had first come to Sheffield had complained of the flowers in their garden catching her dress. More than twenty years had passed since then. Sally was not married and her life was filled by her work in the sewing room at Coles, by attendance at the meetings of the austere sect of the Plymouth Brethren to which she belonged and to the maintenance of her flat. At this stage in my life I had never been up to the top of the stairs to the uppermost flats; it is still quite a taxing physical effort to climb stairs. I had heard my mother and granny describe how all the furniture gleamed from constant polishing, everything was immaculate and the whole place stank of furniture polish.

Across the landing from Sally's flat was the top flat on our side, which was occupied by a mother and daughter. The mother was a dignified and cultured old lady who seldom came downstairs, for she had a weak heart. Her daughter, Minnie, worked for the National Provincial Bank at George Street; this of course is now part of the National Westminster Bank. She was a very bright, lively girl, a committed and dedicated Christian, who was involved for a long time in the Daisy Walk Mission in Saint Philip's parish, which was concerned with spreading the gospel and helping the circumstances of people living in a very poor part of Sheffield, a 'deprived' area in today's jargon (but that was a word we had never heard of). She was also involved in the YWCA, which had its headquarters in a building opposite Walshs.

She was very kind to me and always remembered my birthday with a card

George at the age of about 8 years

and some small present. She gave us Christmas presents of cakes and pastries and I remember one year she gave me a Boy Scout diary. But I never used it as a diary and I don't think I ever made use of the various practical hints in it – like how to cook a hedgehog by covering it with clay so that all the spines came out when it was done. I do remember that at the bottom of every page there was a head and shoulders portrait of a famous person and a quotation; one picture was of Lord Byron and there was a verse:

Man may rule the worst
By ever daring to be first

In those days it was only rich people who went abroad for their holidays but Miss Minnie went to the continent most years after the First World War. She had been born in India – how long she had stayed we never knew but she always spoke of going back. It was generally assumed that her father had served in the army and had died in India, and that had forced his widow and daughter to come to England. We could always recognize her step on the stairs, for whether going up or down she seemed to rush along as if there was not a moment to lose.

I have now described the other tenants in our passage as they were in 1920, the year I started school. From now on my knowledge of the flats, the streets near to them, and wider and wider areas of Sheffield grew and not only by the superficial business of walking into new areas. Rather, as I grew older shapes and things that my eyes had seen but which had been nothing to me seemed to change shape, to stand out and assume new forms; it was as if a mist was clearing from my eyes.

# CHAPTER SIX

# A Church School

I have no idea how it came about that I did not start school until I was 8 and then at the Cathedral school in Queen Street instead of Bow Street school, which was almost in sight of the flats. I remember my mother taking me on the first day. Just as in a dream you suddenly find yourself somewhere, so it was on this first day of my school career. We went from the street into a stone-flagged hallway and a heavy wooden door closed behind us. There was another mother there, but she was alone; she had come to see one of the teachers. We seemed to wait for a while and I noticed a flight of stone steps leading up to a landing. The stairs had a metal rail on the left hand side going up. The other mother was talking to my mother about how she had come to tell off the teacher who had punished her girl; she wasn't going to stand for it.

Then a small dried-up woman with a lot of coarse red hair appeared and I can't remember whether she came down the stairs or not. Anyway, she and the other woman immediately plunged into an argument, but what the outcome was I don't know because just then a door in the hall near the staircase opened and another teacher came out. There was a mighty waft of the smell of plasticine and in the room behind the teacher I could see a lot of boys and girls sitting at desks using their fingers to mould shapes. I was taken and put at a desk and given some plasticine but I don't know what I made with it.

It was in the same room that a teacher introduced us to the Twenty-third Psalm and I was puzzled then and afterwards by 'Thou hast anointed my head with oil'. How could this be? Yet 'Yea, though I walk through the valley of the shadow of death, I will fear no evil' gave me a feeling of comfort for though I didn't know what was meant by 'death' I knew that in our family and where we lived death was often spoken of as being among us. There was another phrase from these early scripture lessons that stuck in my memory and that was 'The lusts of the flesh'. What could they be? What were lusts?

The school seemed a huge place to me. It was on two storeys but for a long time I remained on the ground floor. The room where I worked plasticine and listened to the story of Moses and the bulrushes led into a very big room which was usually divided into three by partitions of glass and wood that slid on metal tracks. Going through this big room I was put in a small room at the end. Here there was a big, beautiful dolls' house and an imposing rocking horse. These lovely toys were for the use of the infants' class to which at first I was confined. How long I remained with the infants I have no idea, but while I was there I was delighted by one of the teachers reading *Uncle Remus* to us. When it ended I was sorry to part with Brer Rabbit.

Next I found myself in a class reading a book about a journey on the moors where there were birds crying 'peewit'. This was a very important moment in my life for I had to hold the book very close to my eyes to see the print and in any case the windows were set very high up so that the light was not all that good. Next thing I was sent to the school clinic for spectacles. In those days the clinic was in Hawley Street where a number of our flats were being used for medical purposes. They all stank of the typical hospital mixture of disinfectant, drugs and bandages. In no time at all I was equipped with a pair of spectacles, the first of many. The optical department was in an upstairs flat and as I descended the stairs they had a frightening tendency to move up towards me.

The journey to the clinic improved my knowledge of the geography of the flats, for this part had been in the misty distance looking down from our part of the yard on the brow of the hill. The Hawley Street flats ran parallel to a large building which most people still called the Jungle. This was because at one time there had been a menagerie there but the City Council had later taken it over for use as a bus garage.

But to return to the Cathedral school . . . I was now aware that the school was in the shape of a letter L. The long side ran along Queen Street, with the door by which I had first entered matched by a similar door at the other end where the building ran up towards the Wolstenholme Hall, which was also owned by the church. This second door led through a bleak draughty hall to a left-hand turn up a flight of stone steps. Here another stairway led to the floor above while to the right was the short arm of the L-shaped building. It was to be years before I saw much of this part of the ground floor, or of the whole upper floor, which was where the older children up to the age of 14 years were taught. There was a concrete playground behind the school bounded by the walls of the adjoining properties. This was divided in two by a brick wall which was used in a game called 'Captain Ball', which involved a ball about the size of a football

George at the age of about 8 or 9
years

being thrown back and forth over the wall. I wasn't interested in games so
although there seemed to be two teams involved I don't know if there were
winners or losers.

Apart from forming up in lines to go to our classes, we also performed
'drill' and marching and counter-marching. Unlike a lot of playgrounds,
ours could not be seen from the street so we never had our parents
watching us. Some time after I got my specs I nearly lost them and an eye.
It happened in the playground during playtime. I was running through the
space at the end of the brick wall when I collided with another boy called
Freddie running in the opposite direction. For some reason he had a pen in
his hand and the nib struck the side piece of my glasses and broke it off and
I felt the nib scrape my face, but luckily it missed my eye.

Apart from Freddie, who I recollect was the son of a barber, I can't
remember much of my fellow pupils but I can recall something of the

teachers. The lady with coarse red hair whom I saw on my first day retired soon after I started. I stood among the other children feeling numb; I didn't know what retirement was and I was puzzled to see the red-haired lady brush tears from her eyes. Earlier I had heard her reproving a Jewish boy, one of two brothers. The younger boy called Reuben was very good-looking and smart but his elder brother was a fat, lazy lad with a dull face. 'I know your mother,' said Redhead. 'She's a very hardworking woman and if you don't work harder she's going to be very disappointed.'

Most of the time the headmaster, Mr C., stayed upstairs with the older pupils and our floor was under the control of a lady whom I suppose was his deputy. I was now a monitor responsible for filling the inkwells and various other minor jobs that gave me a feeling of importance. This I did early in the morning, at playtime and sometimes at the end of school. One playtime I was in the classroom and the deputy head was sitting at her desk, a big thing raised from the floor on a sort of platform so that it was as if she were on a throne. Another teacher came in and stood by the desk and the two of them started talking in low voices. Suddenly the deputy seemed to raise her voice and say something in a sharp tone. To my horror, the other woman started crying. She made a blubbing noise and it seemed to last a long time. I wanted to run away but I thought I would be noticed if I did, so I stayed rooted to the spot. I felt as if I couldn't trust anything any more – children cried, mothers cried, sometimes I cried if I was in pain, but teachers never cried.

The lady who was the deputy head had a sister who also taught at our school. More than twenty years later when I was a grown man I heard that they had both been killed in the Sheffield Blitz of December 1940.

Another memory of something that was disquieting at the time is of a clear, sunny day in the classroom. It was empty except for me and I was quietly putting out books on the desks. Outside there was a lot of noise from the playground. A door opened and the headmaster came in with another teacher, both of them with cold, stern faces. With them was a boy older than me, whom I knew by sight. Not a word was spoken, the three stopped in front of the big desk; the headmaster opened a cupboard and brought out a cane. Still without a word the boy held out each hand in turn, the cane swished time after time, the boy gasped, grunted and went red in the face. Then silently as before the three left the room, with the boy holding his hands in his armpits. It seemed to me that this boy must have committed some terrible crime to be punished like this in secret. I never heard anything to explain the occurrence; like the case of the weeping teacher it remained a mystery.

Among the teachers was a tall, pretty young woman who had a mass of rich, copper-coloured hair hanging in a plait down her back. Realizing I was a budding bookworm she used to lend me copies of *My Magazine, Peoples of All Nations* and odd volumes of *The Children's Encyclopedia* all of which I think were edited by the tireless Arthur Mee.

Starting school brought an end to one of my friendships, that with Teddy. My Teddy was a small yellow-khaki-coloured figure with a soft cuddly body and little floppy ears. He must have been passed on from someone else, for he seemed to have had a lot of use and had only one leg and I seem to recollect that he lost an eye while I had him. I was very fond of him and yet it is only now that the memory of him returns. That is not so with something that I loved even more and clung to after I became a man, retaining it in a cupboard in a shamefaced sort of way. This was a horse mounted on wheels. It was about 18 inches long, standing on a board, with four little wheels to render it mobile. The figure of the horse was very lifelike, with real hair on its head and tail and an air of equine grace, evidently a riding horse for it had a saddle. There was something about this horse, it seemed a living thing patiently waiting for me, so that I hadn't the heart to part with it. Many years later when I left the flat, it seemed foolish, childish, babyish to take it with me so I wrapped it in a lot of newspaper and took it into the pantry and pushed it as far as I could under the stairs. It may have been bought for me by my Uncle George William. Perhaps some archaeologist of the future will find it and speculate that the flat dwellers belonged to a horse-worshipping cult.

At school, eventually I moved into a class in the short part of the L, next to the staircase. I had heard the children in this classroom making a strange rhythmic sound which I discovered when we started to make the same sound was the metric system:

Ten millimetres one centimetre
Ten centimetres one decametre

etc, etc, and despite this I still have to refer to a book every time I run up against the wretched system.

Going to school took me out of the flats. For the first time I became aware of the greatness and variety of Sheffield – how the seamy, ugly, dirty side of the city was redeemed by the spectacular views, the variety of the landscape, riven by valleys beneath stony ridges and steep hills, where mean houses and, much later, tower blocks, assumed a dramatic quality as they stood out against the sky, whether in daylight or shimmering with lights in the darkness of a winter night. Even in my schooldays as I looked at the distant buildings of the city ascending in all directions, words of something I

High Street, Sheffield, *c.* 1900

had been taught at school would float into my mind: 'The strength of the hills is His also.'

The way to the school took me to the end of our block of flats, then I would cross the top of Hawley Street and to my left I would see the other block, the Hawley Street Flats, which we regarded as being inferior to ours. They were built on a different principle. Whereas ours were built with the passage as a unit, these were constructed as a series of decks one above the other and it meant that there were always people passing their front doors.

I then approached the steep descent called Silver Street; right at the corner of the Hawley Street Flats was a kosher butcher's shop and as I started to go down Silver Street I passed the synagogue and then an alleyway where a blacksmith plied his trade. Then it was down past the Three Tuns public house, which was shaped like a flat iron. To my left was spare ground running up to the flats and to the Jungle. This was where in my last year at school, 1926, I saw the ground peppered with holes where men in shirtsleeves were digging for coal in the year of the General Strike and the great Coal Strike.

Then from the Three Tuns across the road to Parkers the builders' merchants, whose premises adjoined our school on one side. There always seemed to be a cold wind blowing here, particularly noticeable when I was on my way back from school. Then past the faded paintwork of the Wolstenholme Hall and round the corner and into school.

Immediately opposite were the premises of Nortons the plumbers' merchants where once they had a fire. How bad it was we never knew, for the school windows were too high up for us to see and in any case we were marched into the playground. We could see nothing but we could hear the voices of the firemen and we heard that some of the teachers were shocked by the strong language used by their chief. Even if we had heard him we wouldn't have understood what he said.

Next to the school was the paint shop of Credlands, with drums and tins of paint emitting a strong, heavy odour. If I arrived early for school in the morning or when I came back after the lunch break I would sometimes walk past Credlands to the street junction where Paradise Street finished and joined Queen Street. I did this because some of the older boys ran up Paradise Street towards Paradise Square, Sheffield's only eighteenth-century square, to exchange insults and sometimes blows with the boys from the private middle class school there. This school was in a building where John Wesley had preached during that period of forty or fifty years when Paradise Square, or 'Pot Square' as it was also called, was a centre for religious and political demonstrations.

# CHAPTER SEVEN

# VANISHED SHOPS

It was about the time when I started school that I remember going down Townhead Street, crossing the road and turning left and going on Broad Lane to a coalyard that was situated just before the junction with Bailey Street. Here I would get a wooden barrow loaded with a quarter of a hundredweight of coal, wheel it home and then wheel the empty barrow back. In those days, when people were very poor, nearly every commodity could be bought in very small quantities. Looking back I realize that my mother or some other grown-up must have been with me; I wouldn't have been trusted with paying money and crossing the road by myself although there seemed very little traffic in those days.

I didn't go any farther up Broad Lane for several years but now I was taken on a route which was partly the way to my school, but which went further on, to West Bar, and from there up another steep street: Scotland Street. To get to Scotland Street we used to walk through a narrow lane which had houses inhabited mostly by Jews where birdcages hung outside the doors. The birds in them were pets, not destined for the table as in Italy. Here was what at the time seemed an enormous chemist's shop, Dysons, with rows of large bottles holding coloured liquids. Inside the shop the walls were lined with shelf after shelf of wooden drawers, each labelled with strange words that didn't seem to make any sense. Strange smells lingered in the shop and often it seemed to be empty and then the chemist came out of a room at the back where people said he 'made up' the doctors' prescriptions. When he had made up a prescription he would hand over the medicine as a flat oblong package covered in stout white paper which concealed the glass medicine bottle, which was marked with little divisions for doses. We used to go there for remedies against colds and coughs made up by the chemist himself, saving us from seeing the doctor. It was when we were going to the doctors that we went up the hill to his surgery at the corner of Meadow Street. This was in a large old house that had seen better

An aerial view of Crofts Buildings in Townhead Street in 1973

days. He was said to have another surgery where he lived at Andover Street on the way to Pitsmoor on the northern side of Sheffield. At this time, in the early 1920s, the area round Scotland Street, Meadow Street, down to the Royal Infirmary in one direction and to St George's church in the other was packed with houses and shops, the streets teeming with people and animals, a lively, noisy, bustling, warm, friendly place.

Now, too, I was taken all along Campo Lane, passing Silver Street, then Paradise Street, another steep, cobbled street leading to the Square, Queen Street, and then North Church Street, where the second synagogue was situated on the right-hand side going down. When I first used to go with granny and my mother along Campo Lane, that part of it between Paradise Street, North Church Street and Hartshead was quite narrow, for the boundary of the cathedral graveyard came part of the way across the present road. I don't know how long it took to widen the road, all I can remember is finding the road wider. From here the route depended on whether mother and granny were going to work or going shopping. Going shopping we would walk past the plant of the *Sheffield Telegraph* and *Star* and an old-fashioned pub called the Dove and Rainbow, leaving the narrow Figtree Lane, where my mother and granny worked, on the left. Now we were approaching Cockaynes Arcade along a narrow street. On the right-hand side there was a line of small shops.

Here I remember Linleys barber shop. In the window would be Baxter prints and one or two violins, for the barber was a man of culture who played the violin. I believe he also claimed to have shaved King Edward VII when he visited Sheffield. Sadly I never visited Mr Linley until he was on the point of retiring just before the Second World War. My own barber was a man who had a shop on West Bar where I was taken for my very first haircut and to whom I remained faithful until he died quite suddenly halfway through the 1930s.

Farther on towards Cockaynes Arcade was a shop selling artists' materials and stamps and stamp albums. It was a long time afterwards that I got the stamp-collecting bug and ventured inside the shop and found the shopkeeper was an elderly, very deaf and very irritable man. Perhaps his affliction was responsible for his irritability. Next was a place like an office – but there was no indication of the sort of business carried on there. I heard people say that the Poor Man's Doctor practised there. The story, whether true or not I do not know, was that the Poor Man's Doctor was a doctor who had been struck off the Medical Register for some kind of misdemeanour but was said to be a very good doctor and cheaper than the established doctors.

At the beginning of the arcade was a line of thick metal posts to prevent vehicles from getting through, then we were into the arcade itself. We never went in Cockaynes nor even looked in the shop windows, for in those days only the well-to-do went into that kind of shop and bought things.

During my early childhood I seemed to suffer from nose-bleeding a lot and by a peculiar circumstance it happened several times in this arcade. Granny had great faith in a remedy which consisted of pushing a bunch of keys down my back; I think it did really work. I have a vivid recollection of our turning round and walking home, of holding a handkerchief to my nose that grew wetter and wetter with blood, feeling the cold keys on my back and being frightened and having a sense of panic as I walked along between the two grown-ups, with people staring at me and the fear that the blood was not going to stop.

Sometimes our objective was the Shambles across the tramlines from Cockaynes. The Shambles was the name given to the meat and fish market. It was a large building shaped like a flat iron, completely black as if it was made of coal rather than stone. There were two entrances facing us and whichever we chose it meant going through a tunnel into a cool, spacious interior with a high ceiling where the shops and stalls were spread out with no sense of crowding. The butchers were round the walls in shops with

Fitzalan Market in Fitzalan Square, *c.* 1910. These buildings were demolished in about 1930 and replaced with Castle Hill Market

white walls, and in the body of the building were the stalls of the fish merchants, some with marble slabs covered with every variety of fish, and poultry, hares and rabbits hanging from hooks. There were also little stalls where cockles, mussels and other delicacies were spread out with the smell of the viands mingling with the strong odour of vinegar. It was a wonderful building for its purpose and sadly while it may have been replaced it has certainly not been improved upon.

From the Shambles it was a short walk to another vanished market that became a favourite of mine. This was the Norfolk Market Hall, named like a lot of other things in Sheffield after the city's greatest landlord, the Duke of Norfolk. From the street you passed through a vestibule lined with shops and entered the market, where lines of permanent stalls filled the middle of the hall and shops lined the sides. The glass roof made it airy and light although sometimes in hot, sunny weather the atmosphere could be somewhat close. Flower stalls and a fountain midway through the hall seemed to provide a scented, tranquil atmosphere. On those early visits to the Market Hall I didn't see the thing that was to attract me in the future: a secondhand-book stall in the corner on the Dixon Lane side of the building, at the top end, where enormous piles of books were presided over by an old man with an ancient black hat on his head. From the first time I saw him he seemed old and he didn't seem to get much older with the years.

Along the Exchange Street side of the Market Hall I was fascinated by a firm which occupied cellars underneath the building. There were some wide doorways leading down stone steps into the interior. The steps themselves were usually partially blocked by sacks of feeding stuff for pets while windows were filled with cage-birds and fish in tanks. In the cellars were all manner of pet animals for sale – puppies, kittens, rabbits, etc., but of course in those days there were no hamsters.

I was taken into the Rag Market, a few steps farther on and I remember being weighed on the scales, a large apparatus with a chair like a throne in which you sat to be weighed. I was at first frightened by the noise – every stall holder shouting at the top of his voice, the crockery men making a great clattering noise with their plates and the man who sold linoleum letting a roll flow down off the edge of the stall and slapping the material so that it gave a sort of muffled thud.

In winter I remember coming past lines of barrows, each with a flaring acetylene lamp providing a wild theatrical sort of light and the cries of the barrow women, who seemed as numerous as the barrow boys.

I realize now that these expeditions to the market were events laden with fear and emotion for my mother, who was on the alert all the time for her husband, but why it should have been so, I do not know, for he worked at night patrolling the markets. On rare occasions I have ventured into Sheffield's modern markets and I think how squalid, tawdry and litter-strewn they are compared with those I knew from my youth.

CHAPTER EIGHT

# HARD LIVES

Between 1920 when I started school and 1924 when granny died, all the three surviving children of John Ashton passed away. Granny was the last.

A child's day seems endless, a week, let alone a month, seems an eternity and so do those five years appear to me, looking back in 1993 after seventy years. In 1920 it was eight years since my father had walked out, no one spoke of him and I did not know such a person existed. Yet now I wonder that I should have been so incurious because most of the children I played with had fathers whom I came to know by sight.

By now I was 8 and there was a pattern of life in the flat with mother and granny that for all I knew had lasted for ever because by now Uncle George William was just a fading memory. One day a week the rent man would come from the Town Hall, knocking on the passage door and then marching in to collect the money. Every day the milkman would come down the passage swinging his silver-coloured metal can, enter the house and measure a gill of milk into the basin waiting for him; a gill, let me remind you, was a quarter of a pint. Sometimes we had more, two gills, or even a pint, but in those days there wasn't a great sale for milk. I was very fond of our milkman; he was a thin, shortish, wiry man, humorous and good-natured, who wore long leather leggings. While he was serving our passage, his horse would quietly move on with the float to the next one and stand perfectly still while the milkman filled his can up again from one of the two big shining churns on the float. There were others like the coalman and the insurance man and also the 'checkman'. This last provided an early form of hire purchase. The checkman who came to our house had a furniture business at Woodseats. When granny or my mother needed an item of clothing of some expense the checkman would give them a paper to take to some shop where he had an account and a little book in which was entered week by week the payment that had been made towards settling the debt. This of course included an extra charge for the benefit of the checkman. A lot of people in poor districts like ours were dependent on this sort of arrangement for getting new clothes, footwear and household items.

Granny and my mother had an income composed of granny's pension and money they earned from cleaning offices and taking in washing. Granny regarded her pension as something wonderful and she absolutely worshipped the man she believed was responsible for her getting it: 'Lord George', as she called him.

When I was small and had just started to walk, granny and my mother used to clean a suite of offices on Queen Street. The main thing I remember about this place is that there were several flights of stone steps and that the walls were lined with green tiles which had some sort of leaf pattern on them. I remember mother and granny mopping the steps and the landings so that everywhere was damp, and one night I somehow slipped and rolled down the stairs unable to stop myself. I finally rolled off the bottom step but without doing myself much damage.

I remember the offices in Figtree Lane much better. From the street you entered an empty hallway with a door to a cellar at the far end. From the hallway a flight of wooden stairs led up to a landing and then another flight led to another landing. The offices on the first landing, two small rooms and one big one, were occupied by an accountant. On the second landing was a large room used as a laboratory by a metallurgist, a small room which he used as an office and a couple of steps leading to a washbasin and, out of sight and up another step, rather unexpectedly, a toilet. It had no door and consisted of a wooden shelf with a hole in it where people sat with a plunger to activate the flush.

This was the time of 'where there's muck there's money' and of 'King Coal' and in the centre of Sheffield a filthy deposit came from the skies – soot and dust from the chimneys of industry and from tens of thousands of domestic fires. Morning and evening there were thick layers of dust on desks, tables, chairs and windows – windows that were almost opaque with years of grime and dust. In the midst of this, mother and granny could only keep the filth in check, dust removed from a desk would only settle somewhere else.

The accountant looked to be an old man and he was an old man. He looked very stiff, starchy, old-fashioned and correct, a Liberal of the old school when the Liberal Party was in decline, and a staunch Nonconformist. He was a pillar of the local League of Nations movement and was a kind man at heart. I was told that when as an infant they had taken me to work, I cried continually. The old gentleman was working late and I disturbed his concentration, but instead of flying into a rage he came to me with a peace offering – a banana. I hope and believe it worked.

A busy Fargate in 1930

The offices were very curious. When I came to read Dickens I felt sure he would have been at home in the Figtree Lane offices. In one room, two clerks used very tall stools to reach long sloping desks reaching to the window bottoms; these were desks that you felt ought to have had quill pens in the little gutters at the top. This room was heated by an enormous black gas fire that filled the hearth and emitted an odour of gas as if it could not be turned off properly. The other clerk's office was where the typist worked. This had more modern furniture and better light, because the window was not quite as dirty on the outside, but it had the same fusty ventilation as the rest of the office. The accountant's office was quite a big room, with two large desks placed front to front, a large green safe in one corner and a thing like a press which pressed a seal on documents. Everything was covered in dust.

It was rather boring for me when mother and granny were working, for there was nothing I could do to help and the time passed slowly as I sat still and kept quiet. One night in an open drawer I saw the catalogue of the Everyman books published by Dent. I picked it up and as I read the descriptions a whole exciting new world opened before me. But would I ever be able to read these books? It seemed unlikely.

There is one thing more to relate about the offices in Figtree Lane. On this particular morning I had not gone to school for some reason. Granny had got the breakfast ready, as mother was cleaning the offices by herself as she often did. Mother seemed to be late, then footsteps could be heard in the passage, the door opened and she came in. Both her hands were bandaged and her face was white. Early on in the morning she had been working in the offices and decided to push a window up so as to shake a duster out of it. No sooner had the window gone up than the sash cord broke and the sash dropped down, trapping mother's fingers beneath it. She was held prisoner for some time until her shouts were heard and someone came to release her and take her to hospital. No bones were broken but the shock of her experience led to both legs breaking out in ulcers, and for the next twenty-five years or more she suffered from the effects of that morning's incident.

Figures in my life from the very beginning when I noticed only their black skirts when they visited us, were granny's sisters. One of them was Sarah Elizabeth, who died in the workhouse. She was the widow of a bricklayer called Kusick who had died in 1903. In widowhood and poverty she consoled herself with spiritualism. I think one reason granny clung so to my mother and was afraid of what would happen if my mother joined my father was her fear that she too might end up in the workhouse. People have no idea nowadays of the horror and fear that the thought of the workhouse inspired among the poor. Years afterwards, mother told me of how she and granny went to the General Cemetery where Sarah Elizabeth's funeral was to be held when the body had come from Firvale. They went to a chapel in the grounds but discovered too late that the service was at another chapel. They were only just in time to see her coffin disappear into a big hole where paupers were buried in a mass grave.

Granny's other sister, Harriet, died in 1921. I think she was the one who married a drunkard who beat her. I have no recollection of ever seeing her but I remember the house where she lived. It was on Carlisle Street, which in those days was lined on one side with row upon row of slum houses and across the road to the east by factories, lines of blackened walls, and behind them the murky river Don. When granny was alive we must have travelled by tram to the beginning of Carlisle Street and walked the rest of the way, or we rode a little farther past the Coliseum cinema and walked down Upwell Street. Although I don't remember granny's sister Hetty I think she must have been alive when I first went there. All the years I was taken on visits I found it an ordeal walking along the street. There were a lot of unemployed men standing in knots, smoking and talking, and as we approached the conversation would stop and they would all stare at us, trying to reckon up who we were. It was worse still on Sundays when it was fine enough and warm enough to sit on the doorsteps to the street; every step would have been whitened with donkey-stone and the inmates would be sitting on them, talking or shouting to each other and appraising the passers-by.

The street had a forlorn, rundown air – there were no bright colours, only a universal dingy darkness brought about by the peeling of paint and the exposure of rotting wood. The only splash of colour was round the occasional little shop where tin plates fastened to the wall advertised cigarettes and tobacco. There was also a disagreeable smell – indescribable – but sewers, soot, decaying wood, flaking paint and stagnant water from broken drainpipes all contributed.

The first house we went to was in a courtyard. We went from the street up a narrow passage, which was very dark at night, and emerged into the yard in which there were a number of houses – I don't know how many. One had to be careful walking up the passage because the constant movement to and fro of people had worn ruts and deep holes in the path, where water accumulated. At one end of the yard were a number of grim looking water closets. More than one family used each and people had keys to them. When we got in the house one thing I noticed was that the floor was uneven as if it was an earth floor.

Hetty's husband lived for some time after his wife. I remember him as a quiet old man. I think he wore a hat, not a cap, but the thing I remember best is his smell, a sort of sweetish scent caused by a lifetime of taking snuff. He wore a waistcoat stained from top to bottom with snuff. In thinking of him and his snuff-taking I remember it was quite a common practice among workers in industries where there was a lot of dust and fumes to take snuff to try to unbung their noses. I don't know if there was any connection with this practice, but in the 1920s it was not uncommon to see men who had lost their noses; it always made me uncomfortable to look at a man with only two holes in his face. Fortunately Hetty's husband's nose was perfect. One thing he described stuck in my memory: a nightlong drinking session which had ended in Exchange Street near the markets. By then he was so drunk that he couldn't stand up and had been forced to creep on all fours down into the Wicker, along the Wicker, up Spital Hill and finally down Carlisle Street.

There was a woman sometimes there who filled me with horror as a child; she was Hetty's daughter and the first time I saw her she had her back to me. She turned round to look at me and, oh, she had only one eye, where the other should have been there was only a hole. I was later told that this woman had left her husband to live with a miner, by whom she had several children. She and her lover had fierce quarrels and I suppose they both drank. In one quarrel they progressed from words to violence and the miner threw a knife at her. It hit her in the eye, destroying the sight, but she shielded him so that the police were never involved.

The management of the household now devolved upon a granddaughter, Ethel. She was a girl with a great deal of personality who arranged for her grandfather, herself and her younger brother to move into a house on the street which was a considerable improvement on the house in the courtyard. We kept in touch with Ethel after granny died but by the middle 1930s we had lost contact. She had a fiery temper like granny and I remember her saying of a row with a neighbour: 'I raised the street on her' – said in a whisper because she had lost her voice shouting.

Ethel may have married the young Irishman who formed the subject of her conversation on the last few occasions we saw her. 'He's very sarcastic!' she would say, laughing. I must say that when we no longer went to Carlisle Street I missed the walk we used to take from there to the Wicker Arches and so home, saving the tram fare. Halfway down the hill there was a space, an opening in which was a chip shop in a wooden van body, which sold the most appetizing fish and chips I have ever eaten. They were wrapped in old newspaper, greasy, wet with vinegar and seasoned with really salty salt. This chip shop was situated near the stables where the railway horses were kept; the big patient dray horses led by men with long shiny aprons.

CHAPTER NINE

# NEW HORIZONS

My mother's half-sister, Susannah, who lived on a farm outside Leicester and had been so good to us during the Great War, invited us to visit her not long after the war ended. It was very kind of her and Uncle Bob to want us to come, for they were still grieving for the death of their only son in the war. I think I must have been asleep during the train journey to Leicester on the London and North Eastern Railway, the LNER, formerly the Great Central. This was the first of many such journeys and the names of the stopping places came to form a tune in my head: 'Nottingham, Loughborough, Leicester, London'. During many years I came to love Sheffield Victoria, with its long impressive approach, its wide concourse, the long hall with stairways leading to the trains, the great rumbling noise of the trains overhead and the spacious platforms – and now it is all gone.

I had lived my short life in the centre of a city, and now for the first time I encountered the country. As I say, I remember nothing of that first train journey. My first memory is of walking in total darkness with each hand held by an unseen adult. From out of the darkness came strange sounds and scents, the smells of grass and dung, the movement of unseen animals, the barking of a dog, the sense of walking on uneven surfaces, sometimes grass, sometimes earth and stones and being lifted over fences. Next I remember coming down some stairs into the farm kitchen where there was a hazy golden light from an oil lamp. There was a table loaded with food, a great piece of cheese, a semi-circle, of what kind I cannot remember for my eye was taken by an enormous egg custard, not only big but deep, a lovely yellow colour with brown blotches here and there. I remember waking in the morning in the room I shared with my mother. It seemed to be high up, at the top of the house, and now as the sun shone through a window too high up to see through, I could hear some more strange noises, buckets rattling and being filled with water, the jingling of harness, the sounds of wild birds and domestic fowls, horses' hooves, cows mooing. I should know what it all meant in time but not just then. Just then it was immensely exciting.

Was it that same day that I walked up the side of a field, a wheat field, and the wheat was taller than me? There was what seemed an enormous covered yard in the middle of which were some geese who hissed at me, but I was safe because Uncle Bob was with me, a big man who was always calm and kind. Uncle Bob gave me a basket and I think he had a pail and he led the way along one side of the covered yard into a series of little rooms in which fowls were nesting and we gently felt inside the nests and took the eggs; all these rooms seemed to smell of straw and there was a lot of it mixed with feathers in the rooms. Another time on a terribly hot day we went to a field where there was an old singledecker tram which had had a stove put in it with a chimney through the roof. I was used to the sight of trams in Sheffield but I was puzzled by this one. What was it doing there? To shelter the farm men, I was told.

Uncle Bob took me to the stables and lifted me up so that I was on a level with the head of a shire horse.

'Would I like to sit on his back?' he asked.

'No,' I said. 'I wouldn't like to sit on his back.'

I tried not to show it, but I was frightened of this great beast. Another time I was shown a large pond where nearly all the surface was covered by a green scum. I don't know, but I think it was another day when I came to look at it again and someone rushed up and said Aunty Susannah thought I had fallen in the pond. Perhaps it was then also that someone showed me how to make daisy chains.

It will be remembered that mother's brother Jim had gone to Leicester to find work, followed by his brother Ted. Ted moved on to Ashby-de-la-Zouch but Jim stayed in Leicester and married. While we were at the farm it was decided to visit Uncle Jim, who lived in the Belgrave district of Leicester. Of course, I don't remember how I came to be sitting in a chair at Uncle Jim's dinner table but I do remember one incident very clearly. Uncle Jim's wife Nance was a wonderful cook. In fact, she had been the cook to a wealthy family. She was a good wife and made us welcome. She was, however, a woman with a sharp tongue and very little patience with her husband who was already having trouble with his hearing and would eventually become almost stone deaf. In short, Aunt Nance was a waspish character and there I was seated on a chair with my small legs dangling while everybody tucked into a beautiful meal. But suddenly I disturbed the proceedings by howling at the top of my voice. No one could understand why I was howling until someone looked under the table and discovered that Aunt Nance's pet pom, a spoilt, overfed, disagreeable beast, had got my toe in its jaws. I have often heard it said that dogs grow like their owners; I certainly had an object lesson very early in my life.

Just after the Great War ended and I started school, a new pleasure entered granny's life. There was a woman who lived in a ground-floor flat in the next passage, which was the first passage in Townhead Street. This woman worked at one of the cinemas, picture palaces they were called, which had gradually spread through the city from before the war. This one was called the Albert Hall in Barker's Pool; it was a massive brick building originally used as a concert hall and boasted a celebrated organ. Granny's friend in the next passage was in charge of the usherettes at the cinema and she induced the manager to send the dirty towels used in the cloakrooms and staffrooms to our flat to be washed.

Apart from the small amount of extra income this brought in, it meant that we all became eligible for complimentary tickets and were able to see the films every week. Granny liked the pictures but mother had to read all the subtitles to her. There were a lot of people at that time who could not read and like granny were dependent on a literate companion to make sense of the film. These were silent films, of course, but a steady hum of voices accompanied the moving pictures and could be heard above the musical accompaniment which at the Albert Hall was sometimes an orchestra.

The very first occasion I can remember being in the Albert Hall with granny and mother I remember nothing of the film, but I know we were sitting on a wooden bench in the balcony. Ever afterwards, though, my memories are of sitting downstairs on tip-up seats in the stalls. Next I can remember scenes from two different films; one was in a church, it was dark and gloomy with candles burning and there was the body of someone lying raised up on something – 'lying in state', people said. The other scene that I never forgot was in what must have been a Cavaliers and Roundheads film; in this scene, several men were fighting with swords in a room. One man thrust at another with his sword, it went in the front of the other man's body and stuck out at the back. I was stunned. I had always thought people were like walls, that nothing would go through them.

Long after granny died, my mother continued to wash the towels of the Albert Hall – in fact until it was burned down – so I saw hundreds of films, silent and talkies. So now I am not sure which I saw with granny. One I am sure we all three went to see was called *Fires of Fate*, based as I now know on a story by Arthur Conan Doyle called *The Tragedy of the Korosko*. With my talent for remembering oddments from films I remember a character saying: 'It's dangerous to go beyond Wadi Halfa.' There was a happy ending brought about by the Egyptian Camel Corps. We all enjoyed it and I remember walking along and looking back at the Albert Hall all ablaze with light at night and across the front a large poster which read: 'Wanda Hawley in *Fires of Fate*.'

Another film I remember was called *The Covered Wagon*, which was about the early settlers in the Wild West. The manager of the Albert Hall, a man of infinite resource and imagination, had men dressed as cowboys and Indians on the stage at the side of the screen as an introductory attraction. Another time, when *The Prisoner of Zenda* was being shown, the theatre foyer was transformed into the courtyard of a castle with two mounted lifeguards resplendent in jackboots, breastplate and helmet and one man mounted on a real live horse. Another time, when a war film about the Battle of Ypres was being shown, there was another transformation, this time to trenches with sandbags, a dugout, barbed wire, and dummy soldiers all bathed in a dim green light. This manager had served in the navy during the war and he made headlines in the local paper by walking the wings of a biplane over Sheffield. The Albert Hall was also the venue for concerts, and had its own orchestra under an Irish conductor. This orchestra seemed to have a rather limited repertoire consisting of three pieces by Suppé: *Light Cavalry, Poet and Peasant* and *Morning, Noon and Night in Vienna* and a piece called *The Storm* in which the celebrated organ joined in. There was a concert I particularly remember when the hit tune of the moment was *Yes! We have no Bananas*. As a stunt the manager sent people on the stage in front of the screen with bunches of bananas which they broke into single pieces and threw into the audience. This was in the early 1920s when the saxophone had become a very fashionable instrument. At one concert the programme consisted almost entirely of four men playing different sizes of saxophone and their music stands were draped in red and gold hangings; we really felt terribly modern, although none of us liked the sobbing sound of the instruments.

Another of granny's pleasures for which she needed my mother's aid was in following murder trials in the newspapers, particularly the *News of the World*. Apart from 'Lord George', or Lloyd George, whom she thought had been responsible for awarding her a pension, her other great hero was Sir Edward Marshal Hall, the famous advocate, who specialized in defending hopeless cases. I can remember my mother reading at night by the gaslight long reports of trials and the latest murders. Granny loved a good murder and there seemed to be plenty of them in those days, such as Thompson and Bywaters, the Green Bicycle Case, and others. She and my mother followed a case that was not a murder; this was the Russell case in which an aristocrat claimed that the son his wife bore had not been fathered by him; the case seemed to go on for ages.

Memories of the past shoot up like mushrooms out of the dark backward of time. During the last year or so of granny's life there were still people about who seemed like survivors of an earlier day, like the muffin man with his basket or the knifegrinders with their curious machines which they wheeled round the yard. Actually very few knives were brought for sharpening, it was mostly scissors. Then there was a youngish woman who came round selling watercress who was accompanied by a little girl. The watercress woman was very thin and had a paper-white face; she seemed weak, almost at death's door. She told my mother her husband had deserted her and left her to bring the little girl up by herself. I think mother had a feeling of kinship with this woman and saw a parallel between them, both had a child and no husband, and so she always bought the watercress. After a time the woman ceased coming. She reappeared several weeks later hardly able to crawl and after that we never saw her again. Mother said she must have died.

Another visitor to the flats in the early 1920s was a scruffy-looking elderly man who was very simple and mentally retarded. I remember him because when it rained he would hold his hands out and say, as if he had discovered a great truth, 'Rain put fire out!'

I don't remember religious meetings in the flats at this time, but I remember a couple of political meetings while granny was alive. As it happened both were organized by the Labour Party. Once the main speaker was a woman. The meeting was held in the yard against the dividing wall and right opposite our flat. The lady speaker was a very excitable person who kept jumping up and down on the wall and as she did so shouted hysterically and waved her arms. Another time a politician with a German name came seeking votes. In the course of his speech he chanced to say: 'Here you live like pigs.' This phrase enraged a fiery little woman who lived in one of the middle flats on the Hawley Street side.

'Do you say we're pigs?' she screamed.

The speaker tried to explain what he really meant but met such a stream of interruptions that he hurriedly collected his papers together and beat a hasty retreat with his followers. I think he was afraid the little woman might come down into the yard and assault him with more than words.

My granny loved Lloyd George but was deeply sceptical of all politicians, Tory, Liberal or Labour, whom she regarded as all feathering their own nests.

In spite of a hard life granny's health had been good. She was now well past 70, which was a milestone a lot of poor people never reached. She was thin and bony with a stern expression and outside the house she still wore her old-fashioned bonnet and I think used a stick. Now, however, she was taken seriously ill with erysipelas, which affected her not only physically but mentally; she would not let my mother do anything for her; everything had to be done by the cinema lady from the next passage. Her last illness didn't last very long. In no time at all it seemed she was dead, during the early hours of 15 July 1924. I suppose all the business of 'laying out' the body would have been carried out by a couple of the wise women living in the flats who went regularly to perform that task, visiting one flat after another. My mother and I got up early in the morning. Mother was silent, grieved that what she had long feared had occurred and that now she was alone, the woman she had always thought of as 'Mother' gone. I felt a great surge of love and sympathy for my mother. The early morning seemed dull and bleak like the future. I tried to comfort her and said she still had me and I would look after her.

It was at granny's funeral that the mourners travelled to City Road Cemetery in a sort of horse bus. At previous funerals we had had a carriage, rather like a cab, but this time, to save money, I suppose, we got into this long narrow vehicle with a wooden bench on each side. Following the big black hearse it took a long time to get to the cemetery as it was uphill all the way and the horses couldn't hurry. A Mr Thirsk had made the coffin, but whether he had supplied the horses and so on I don't know. He called himself an undertaker then, if he were living today he would be a funeral director.

Now there was only my mother and me. If I could only get a job when I left school – any sort of job so long as I had a little money to help her – then I should be content. I had no idea what lay beyond school. I had no ambition, or any idea of what I wanted to be. I had a feeling that I was someone without luck.

# CHAPTER TEN

# FINAL SCHOOLDAYS

By the time granny died my world had opened out in all directions. I knew the flats and most of the area around us. There were a lot of children in the flats and I knew many of them. We played games like hide-and-seek and cowboys and Indians. In this last game we galloped up and down the passages on imaginary horses and when we came to the end of the passage where there were steps into the yard, we used to jump over them to make as much noise as possible.

One woman lent us a large piece of carpet and this was our boat floating on the sea — we camped on it, eating sweets and being careful to stay on it lest we fall into the salty waves.

Tommy, Mary and I from our passage, and a few others, used to play a less strenuous game with some of the children in the middle and top flats of Hawley Street. They used to come to the end of their verandahs and we played what I suppose was really charades, but we called it something else. One of us performed some action supposed to represent the name of something. Mostly I still played with Young Tom at 90, he had a great many games we could play and also a large army of toy soldiers, and we had battles and parades.

In the Hawley Street passage that faced us across the yard lived an old Jewish man and his wife. After a while they left and the people who followed them grumbled that the boiler in the kitchen had been used for cooking fish in olive oil. They were followed by some people who had a boy with flaming red hair. Before I could get to know him, he and the family emigrated to Western Australia, but not for long. They returned in what seemed a short while with stories of the difficulty of buying crockery and of killing snakes in the barn.

In the next passage, where the lady who worked at the Albert Hall lived, the top flat on her side was occupied by a man who was a porter at the Royal Hospital. I thought this must be a very important job. He had one boy and several girls and the younger ones used to come down to play with us. The Albert Hall lady was married to a retired policeman, a big, bulky man who came out on occasions to move us children on if we were being mischievous. We were rather frightened of him. In those days a mother had only to say 'I'll fetch the Bobby to you!' for order to be restored immediately.

The ground-floor flat in the next passage nearly opposite the British Legion club was associated in our minds with a very alarming event. The woman who lived at this flat answered a knock at the door to find a gypsy woman on the threshold selling various oddments such as clothes pegs. She refused to buy anything, so the gypsy woman looked angry, gave her a piercing glance and said: 'You're a bad woman and you'll come to a bad end before the month is out.' A week later the housewife was dead. Needless to

Sambourne Square in Edward Street, c. 1910. These houses were built in around 1790. Mrs Yates, a midwife, stands in her doorway on the left

say, after that as soon as the word spread that gypsies were in the vicinity everybody locked their doors and hid inside. I suppose it was a 1920s manifestation of the fear of the evil eye.

In one of the upstairs flats lower down Townhead Street there lived a boy who was mentally retarded. I am sorry to say that we thoughtless children used to delight in tormenting him if we saw him on the verandah of their flat. Some of the family coal stock was kept on the verandah and our object was to annoy him so much that he would throw lumps of coal at us. The same boy used to lean out of the bedroom windows that faced the street and try and spit on passers-by. He had a relative, a cousin I think, who used to visit the family from time to time. He sang in a church choir and later on had a most distinguished career singing alto in several cathedral choirs. I remember one occasion when this cousin came to visit clad in what we thought were quite outlandish garments. He caused a sensation when he appeared in the yard dressed in what one of the grown-ups said was the Eton College outfit. Of course Freddie did not attend Eton, so I suppose it was the uniform of a local private school.

In the 1920s one of the things I saw from my bedroom window on a Sunday was the procession of housewives to the Golden Ball as noon approached. They were going to fetch jugs of beer to accompany Sunday dinner. A few of the ladies marched back boldly, holding their jugs for all to see, but the majority concealed the jug under a shawl or a towel – the jugs themselves, I recollect, were big ones with bright floral patterns. The shawl was then a very common item of female attire, draped round the shoulders or covering the head completely save for the eyes.

There was a pianist at the Golden Ball who lived somewhere on the flats. She was a middle-aged, good-hearted, usually slightly tipsy woman who used to greet me through our window and would try to push pennies through the window frame to me. She had a brother who seemed slightly odd. Clad in mackintosh and cap he would stand for hours under our window, discoursing to his niece – whether on politics or religion I never knew. The girl never opened her mouth but listened passively, the only break occurring when there was a momentary traffic jam, a rare occurrence in those days, when he would step into the road to direct traffic.

On Sunday also there would be a gathering of the young bloods of the district under our window. The central figure would be a young man whose parents kept the pork shop in West Bar. He would ride up on a 'Daisy' motorbike and for the rest of the evening would sit astride his bike enjoying the attention of his cronies. Motorbikes were not all that common in our district and I used to sit on my table hoping he would start his machine and ride up and down, but he never did until it was getting dark.

On Sundays too as the time of the evening service at St James' approached I would watch for the vicar, Mr Parsons, coming from his vicarage near the Jessop Hospital. It was quite a walk and he would arrive, coat tails flying, but with his shiny top hat securely fixed on his head just before the time of the evening service. As he came out of Trippet Lane he would produce a final burst of speed that took him to the church door with a couple of minutes to spare.

As early as I can remember, and until the Second World War, the newspapers were delivered by a stout, weather-beaten woman who came with the morning, evening and Sunday papers. She brought them in a big wooden barrow, probably home-made, which had metal tyres, so that you could hear its progress for a long time before it came in sight. She had an astonishing memory for customers and prices, never writing anything down but always knowing what papers each person had and how much they owed. Besides the barrow she always carried two great bags full of papers. She seemed to bring the family with her, and as the children grew up they were promoted to delivering papers to the upstairs flats. Her ability to keep track of her customers' requirements and debts was all the more remarkable because all the time she was engaged in a continuous argument with an invisible adversary, presumably her husband, 'chuntering' away all the time. She started work early but when the theatres and cinemas were turning out she would still be selling her papers, sheltering in shop doorways from the wind, cold and rain.

Now I return to my schooldays. I think that with starting school three years later than anyone else, I was pushed rapidly through the infant classes – more rapidly than, looking back, it seems to me now. So I went to the upper floor where the headmaster reigned from an enormous desk, much bigger than that of the deputy head on the ground floor. When we arrived in the morning we had what would nowadays be called assembly. We used to go into a middle room, say prayers and sing a hymn. The Jewish children at the school used to wait outside the door while we performed this ritual. I think that, like the children in the infant classes, we used to hold our hands out for inspection to see if they were clean. As we massed in this Assembly and later took our places in the class I could smell some boys with a lavatory sewage smell, and there were others who had holes in their trouser bottoms from which bits of shirt stuck out.

At other times during the week we used to sing *Cherry Ripe* and *Come Lasses and Lads*. After a very short time I ceased to play an active part in the singing. Our headmaster was quite a noted choirmaster. He used to conduct the church choirs in the Whitsuntide sing and he used to go down the ranks for 'groaners'. He detected one in me and commanded me to stop singing, a command I have obeyed during the last sixty years.

Smithfield, *c.* 1930

At Christmas, the partitions on the upper floor were rolled back, creating one big room into which the whole school was massed, to be joined by a trio of instrumentalists with whom the pupils took part in Hely-Hutchinson's setting of *Nursery Rhymes*. At Easter we marched in procession up the steep cobblestones of Paradise Street and Paradise Square to the cathedral, crossing the widened Campo Lane to get to it.

After moving from the Lower School I found myself in a class where they were reading Scott's *A Legend of Montrose*, and learning Portia's speech from *The Merchant of Venice*. I was fascinated by Walter Scott and Dugald Dalgetty, and my interest in history became an obsession.

Children seemed to be always leaving our school or joining it from somewhere else – some school that was overcrowded, as a rule. There were Jewish children among the new arrivals. One Jewish boy was a small, very thin child with bright lustrous eyes. He said he had come from Russia and talked about riding on a sleigh in the cold and darkness, and hearing wolves howling in the forests. Years afterwards I saw that boy's name on a furniture shop and I wondered if it was my fellow scholar. By then I was less innocent than when I was at school and I wondered if he had really been in Russia. There were other Jewish boys and the odd girl and they all seemed immensely more grown-up than we were, and personally I always felt ignorant and innocent compared with them.

The next classroom I was in was at the end of the building where the school ran up against the premises of a builders' merchant. You could get into the classroom from the next one but right at the far end was a door leading to the corner of the school property where some very smelly lavatories were situated and the ground was always wet. Before going out into the open to the lavatories we passed a staircase running up to the laboratory on the floor above the classrooms. Going up these stairs I liked it when we had to wait for a while and could watch the workmen next door wheeling barrows and doing various jobs. When we got into the laboratories it was a different world, very scientific-seeming with delicate balances in glass cases, Bunsen burners, test tubes, water tanks, etc. The teacher in charge of the laboratory sometimes deputized for the headmaster but the children did not like him much because he had a very sharp tongue and a sarcastic one. We used to perform little experiments with acids, being taught the meaning of words like 'oxide' and 'saturation'. It was in the laboratory that we were introduced to the latest idea in education – lessons by radio. I can remember this happening but what lessons we received and what sort of radio was used are blind spots in my memory, which usually remembers things as pictures.

When I moved into the dark classroom on the floor beneath the laboratory, a new teacher who had just arrived was reading *Treasure Island* to the class. It seemed a wonderfully exciting book and we were always sorry when he stopped. The new man introduced us to Shakespeare. He started us on *Henry V* and gave everybody a speaking part. The words when spoken took on a new dimension, we realized they meant something, that there was real life mirrored in the play, the speeches were not flat lines of words on a page to be memorized but emotions and thoughts that had a life of their own. The new teacher who later on became the last headmaster of the school was an inspiring guide to knowledge but we didn't like him much. I was very pleased to be in his classroom all the same. It was dark, but there was a large open fire protected by a massive fireguard upon which I used to sit when I arrived early on a winter morning.

The last Christmas I spent at the school, that of 1925, is a high point in my memory. There was a wonderful Christmas Treat for the whole school in the Wolstenholme Hall. It was an evening event attended by all the teachers, the headmaster and the archdeacon. This archdeacon came to the school quite a lot. He was a tall man with a stoop who left Sheffield to become a bishop and died after he had become an archbishop in Africa. He gave us religious chats as we sat at our desks in the sun-filled classroom. He must have been a shy man, very self-conscious in the presence of children. How otherwise explain his continual moving from place to place in the room, sitting on the edge of one desk after another, now heaving himself onto a table and then pacing up and down. This was the man who made the speech at the commencement of the Christmas Treat and he ended it with the words: 'I hope you eat and eat until you burst!' Although we did our best to comply with the injunction and made great inroads in the piles of delicacies, we had to call a halt before we got to the bursting stage. I remember that one boy who had a good voice sang *Old John Bradlum*, all ten verses of it, from 'Number one, now my song has just begun' to 'Number Ten, If you want any more you can sing it yoursen.'

My schooldays were nearly over but were prolonged because of the General Strike and the long Miners' Strike of 1926. Some months earlier, as my future departure from school drew nearer, the headmaster had told me that he hoped to get me a job at the City Libraries as he had succeeded in doing with another boy a year or so before. I suppose it was only some sort of errand boy's job but it might have led to something better; however, I was soon told that the prospect had vanished.

I was still at school when the 1926 Test series was being played against Australia. The department store, Coles, was then still in the building at the corner of Church Street facing the Cathedral. In anticipation of the Test Match to be played at Headingley a gadget had been placed at the top of the building along the famous Corner. When the Test was played, the latest scores and information appeared in large letters and figures. I and some others used to tramp up from the school instead of going straight home at teatime and sit on the cathedral wall with our backs against the railings that then enclosed the churchyard – railings swept away during the 1939–45 war. I remember the names of some of the heroes taking part in the Test Match – Woodfall and Ponsford for the Australians, and do I remember aright, did Macauley, Leyland and Kilner play? I sat there in the sunshine but that is about all I remember. That summer when there was no Test Match I walked back from school as usual up Silver Street and saw men digging for coal on the open ground below Hawley Street Flats.

I was now at the end of my schooldays and had reached Standard 8 in the spring and summer of 1926. I once more mounted the stairs to the sunny classroom which housed the headmaster's desk in a corner placed in front of a big scroll which bore the words: 'Play Up!, Play Up! and Play The Game.' Maybe it is selective memory but that year 1926 and that classroom seem bright with sunshine.

When I finished school I thought I should never enter the old building again, but twice I returned. During the Second World War, I was summoned there to a Civil Defence lecture on butterfly bombs and how to deal with them. Although the building had ceased to be a school some years before the war, to my surprise the school furniture was still in place although everything seemed to have shrunk. The lecture was held in a small classroom upstairs overlooking the playground. It was, as I remembered, a sunny room, but the desks which I also remembered well were surprisingly small. I had difficulty in sitting down and even more difficulty in extricating myself when the meeting was over. Much later, in about 1960, I found myself once more in the school building. By this time it had become a furniture repository and the ground floor where the infants had been taught and where I had first practised my reading was full of tables, sets of drawers and chairs. Now I regret that I never took any photographs while the building was still intact, for now it has vanished utterly beneath an office block.

# CHAPTER ELEVEN

# SHEFFIELD REVEALED

During the years I was attending school my knowledge of Sheffield increased by leaps and bounds. A lot of it was brought about by trams. Sheffield was proud of its tram service, which was improved and modernized all the time, unlike that of some towns, Leicester for instance, where Edwardian trams were still running in the 1930s. If I woke in the darkness of early morning I would hear the first tram, a faint sound then getting louder and louder until it would rattle across the top of the street into Church Street and gradually fade away. From my position in the window I would see very small single-decker trams going to the steep hills of Walkley, but mostly they were double-deckers.

Sometimes we went by tram to the East End of Sheffield, the steelworks end, and then onto Parkgate, a district of Rotherham where granny had some friends who kept a tobacconist's shop. I disliked going to the East End.

The double-decker trams had an open verandah at each end and for some reason, maybe it was the track, they used to buck up and down and if I sat in the verandah I felt that I might go flying over the ornamental metal sides. At one time I used to like to go downstairs where people sat on two long benches, one on each side, and I would be staring over the glass door onto the driver's platform where he operated gleaming brass handles and wheels. There was one kind of tram that fascinated me because they were said to have come from Paris. They had a lot of highly polished wood with a swirling pattern on the roof.

Small shops predominated at this period of my life. I mean the little grocers' shops where sugar was weighed into thick blue paper bags; flour was stored in big cylindrical drums nearly as big as a man, from which it was weighed out; treacle oozed from taps behind the counter; and butter was in great heaps from which small portions were cut, although in shops like the Home and Colonial and the Maypole the assistants were equipped with paddles with which they made a great slapping noise patting the butter into shape. Our nearest grocer's, which was next to the coalyard and right under the shadow of St James, was where I used to get halfpennyworth's of sweets, that is half an old penny – chlorodynes were my favourites. The lady who ran the shop was lucky in that her husband had returned from the war, but he had come back with only one arm, and it was a great handicap to his helping in the shop. His wife's sister, who sometimes helped in the shop, had lost her husband in the German East African campaign. For a long time I had a German banknote which she gave me, but it is long since lost. Cigarettes such as Woodbines were sold in fives in little shops which were the front rooms of houses.

Once I went on an errand for my mother to the lodging house next door. I remember several single beds in shiny black iron but most of all I remember an odour of chamber pots. Round the corner of the street in Vicar Lane was a door leading into a place belonging to the Church Army, where unemployed men cut timber into firewood and went out with it loaded onto a crude handcart with long handles.

Walsh's shop in the High Street, c. 1932

I knew that walking down Church Street and going round the corner, the narrow 'gennel' then facing me, Chapel Walk, would lead me to two of Sheffield's theatres, the Lyceum and the Theatre Royal. I went with the school to see *Peter Pan* and the strongest memory I have of that production is that there was a man in it dressed as a dog. As regards the Royal, I remember posters advertising *Tons of Money* and other farces. It always looked a shabby sort of place and was eventually burned down.

There were two other theatres in Sheffield, both now only memories, the Empire in Charles Street and the Hippodrome in Cambridge Street. I had been in both of them but my earliest memories were not of the theatres but of incidents in the shows, like a comedian singing a song with a chorus of 'Where do the Flies go in the Wintertime?' and a scene in a pantomime of *Robinson Crusoe* when down the steps from the back of the stage a couple of big men entered clothed in fur, with fur hats on their heads, and over their shoulders they carried big, clumsy-looking guns. Forty years later, I had almost forgotten this pantomime scene when I called to see the agent of a Derbyshire estate. He was out, but as I turned to go he and his son returned from a day's shooting in the woods carrying their guns over their shoulders – suddenly for a moment I was a small boy staring up at the stage in wonder, but these men had no fur coats or hats.

In 1924, at the age of 12, I was eligible to join the library. The Sheffield Central Libraries were then housed in two Victorian buildings on Surrey Street on the same site as the present Graves Building. The building nearest to Arundel Street was the lending library; I am not sure now whether it was this lending library or the reference library adjacent to it and nearer to the town hall which had been a mechanics institute. There was a space between them occupied by a small ornamental garden and from one library to the other the garden background was a high fence with a large board on which improving slogans and messages were displayed. The words that stuck in my mind were something to do with the Elizabethans and said: 'There is no land unhabitable or sea unnavigable.'

The lending library was on a series of levels; entering from the street you went down steps, only a few it is true, but once inside, part of the library was about three steps below the rest. One of the people in charge was a tall, severe-looking man with silver hair. It so happened I had seen a film at the Albert Hall about the Spanish American War, which I found very puzzling, and the next time I was in the library I asked a young woman assistant if there was a book about it. She had a look round without success and then asked Silver Hair and I heard him deliver the following pearl of wisdom: 'Don't bother about it! The smaller the child the bigger the book!' I'm sure he was right.

The reference library was a very awe-inspiring place. One stepped from the street into a cool silent world and climbed up the staircase into a room whose odour and silence suggested a place of worship. There, various corners and recesses were occupied by shelf upon shelf of beautifully bound books. Everywhere there was glistening polished wood and the small number of readers and staff made scarcely a sound, either by voice or by their footfalls on the carpet. It was all like being in a very superior chapel.

After once venturing inside it was years before I went to the reference library again. By then it was in temporary premises near the Lyceum Theatre. Unless I am mistaken, in those days the library was open on Sunday afternoon and it was very pleasant to sit reading there on a warm sunny afternoon when the whole city seemed asleep. This must have been during the time when the present Graves Library was being built.

Going to and from the library and also the Albert Hall cinema I had to go through Leopold Street and pass the steps leading to the Grand Hotel. Just by the steps was a large, important-looking hoarding which had the words 'International Celebrity Subscription Concerts' painted in large letters on the top and usually beneath there would be just one or two words such as 'Kreisler' or 'John McCormack'. If going to the Grand Hotel was a sign that you were wealthy and select, then people who went to these musical events, these feasts of classical music, seemed to belong to an even rarer breed, a true elite. Nobody from our rank in life ever went and in fact there was a feeling that anyone from our background who went to hear that sort of noise must be a silly sort of snob and a traitor to his class.

Apart from the theatres, a lot of popular music and entertainment took place in the chapels and their schoolrooms. There was a chapel at Petre Street where we once went to hear the *Messiah* because one of the ladies whom mother cleaned for sang in the choir. Another time we went on a bus past the wooden huts at Tyler Street where munition workers lived during the Great War. I remember that particular concert because one of the attractions was a man who used his hands to cast all sorts of strange shadows on a screen – the shapes of rabbits, dogs, horses, cats, etc.

I didn't understand chapels; they didn't seem solemn like churches, more like offices. I suppose this was because they had so much polished wood and plain glass. During the period when I was at school and before granny died we were only very occasional attenders at St James's. Mr Parsons, the vicar, gained much praise from the way he handled an unexpected situation which arose in 1921, I think, when a demonstration by the unemployed led to trouble in the streets. The top of the street was black with people and the mothers of the children on the flats were calling us in and locking the doors. Suddenly a lot of men came rushing downhill seeking refuge from

St James' church in Townhead Street in the early 1940s. Note the air-raid shelter in front of the church and the boarded up windows

the police; we could hear people running down the passage. A large crowd turned off Townhead Street, through the churchyard and poured into the church, where Mr Parsons rose to the occasion and conducted an impromptu service for this unexpected congregation.

When I really started to take notice of the district in which I lived after the Great War there was a stability in my immediate world, our passage and the neighbouring passages, but granny's death in 1924 was only one of a series of changes that occurred in the next couple of years.

Young Tom, the boy next door, was my main playmate despite being two or three years older than myself. He was the leader of our gang, the one who planned new games. In summertime his father, Old Tom, used to come into the yard with his son and play cricket using dustbins as wickets. It was a game that demanded discretion; there was always the risk of driving the ball into someone's window. Miss Minnie and her mother, who lived in one of the top flats in our passage, had a nephew called Charlie who lived in Townhead Street. He used to join us and I think some of the girls – Mary, the piano tuner's granddaughter, and the daughters of the hospital porter.

It was soon after granny died that Grace, Young Tom's mother, called us into their flat. She wanted us to look at a long pile of books on their sideboard which she said they had had to buy because they were needed for Young Tom's studies at the secondary school on Leopold Street. It had cost them a lot of money but they grudged nothing so long as Young Tom got the chance of climbing to a better job than his father, of getting a good wage without having to get his hands dirty. We now heard from time to time how well Young Tom was doing at school; every subject seemed to present only opportunities to shine, but it was his art work, painting and drawing that earned him the most praise at the school.

We were told that the art teacher at the school was very impressed with Tom's talent; he was a man who had worked in Paris before the war, so it was said. Tom's mother came to tell my mother that they would be leaving the district at which my mother felt very sad at losing such good neighbours. Grace explained that Tom's art teacher had come to see her and her husband with a proposal that seemed a fantastic, unbelievable stroke of luck for their son. The teacher suggested that he should take Young Tom as his pupil and protégé; he would buy a house in which they would all live and where Grace would be the housekeeper while Old Tom would follow his own occupation. I believe the parents saw the disadvantages of this scheme at once and were inclined to turn down the proposal, but then they thought that they had not the right to stand in their son's way so agreed.

Naturally my mother and I were very curious to see the man who was Young Tom's benefactor when we were told that he walked to the school every morning going past our passage on his way up Townhead Street. I can remember him now as a man who walked in a sort of slow, apathetic, listless gait with a raincoat over one arm and part of it sweeping the ground. He dragged one leg and I was told this was from a war wound which had never healed.

While Tommy was still living across the passage, our mutual friend Charlie came and brought a model sailing ship, which he said was a clipper. He and Tom arranged that the three of us should take it to Millhouses Park and sail it on the pond there; this was after Tom had launched the boat in the kitchen sink of his flat. We caught a tram near the town hall and went what seemed a very long journey to Millhouses. We then walked through the park by the most direct route, crossing streams by fallen trees wherever we could.

Reaching the pond we launched the clipper after Tom had checked the set of the sails. It sailed elegantly to the middle of the pond, then the wind died away and it stopped. The craft remained motionless, so we equipped ourselves with sticks, took up position on three sides of the pond and began furiously churning the water with our sticks. I leaned forward, my foot slipped, the water rose towards me and I fell in with a splash. I was completely surprised, I seemed to fall on my back, I couldn't get up, I was choking, then I felt I was being raised, my head was lifted above the water. I am sure I should have been drowned but for the intervention of an unknown boy. I remember sitting on the bottom deck of a tram, very wet, with somebody's coat round me; on the other side of the tram was my rescuer, but that is all I know of him. I felt stunned, not really there, as if I were looking through a window, then the next thing I was home and being put to bed.

I didn't suffer any ill effects from my experience, indeed I was rather cossetted by my mother and Young Tom's mother. Young Tom's mother brought a thick book, a bound volume of the *Boy's Own Paper*. It had a story in several instalments called 'In the Land of Shame' by Major Charles Gilson about fighting slave traders in Africa, and there were articles about fighting at sea in the Russo-Japanese War and another long story about Henry V and the Battle of Agincourt. What with all this exciting reading matter and the stunned feeling I had about falling in the pond it never occurred to me to ask about the boy who had saved my life.

The departure of my friend Tom was not the only change. One of the lady dressmakers above us died, but the other one stayed on and her sewing machine continued to go bump, bump. In the other middle flat, Mary's grandfather, the old piano tuner, died and left his widow with the sole responsibility for Mary. The first I knew that anything had happened to the old gentleman was when someone brought me a musical instrument he had had – I think it was a zither. It was made of shiny black wood and had a row of white keys for plucking wires; it was damaged and I soon lost patience with it, although with the aid of some instructions I managed to make a noise that sounded like *The Bluebells of Scotland*.

The neighbouring passage on Townhead Street had a change in the larger of the two top flats. The family, whose father was a porter at the Royal Hospital, moved. I think that the father died. They were succeeded by a Catholic family with five children – four boys and a girl.

I don't know how long it was after granny's death that my father appeared. I think he hoped for a reconciliation now that Lucy Ann was dead. I am sure he was right in thinking that my unofficial granny had wrecked his marriage and poisoned his wife's mind against him. I was thunderstruck when this strange man came in the flat one day and I wouldn't shake hands and showed my dislike when he tried to make friends; I suppose I was jealous, there had only been me and granny and mother, and now there was only me and mother; why should there be any change?

Father started coming in the evenings and brought gifts in the shape of bound volumes of *The War Illustrated*. I was fascinated by the books. I used to sit quietly turning the pages while they sat on the horsehair sofa under the living-room window talking in low tones. My father had found the key by which we could have become friends but it was not to be. Like a character in a play I could have said 'Nobody tells me anything!' and now I can only speculate on why my parents failed to resurrect their marriage. I think the sticking point was who's name should be on the rent book, whether of our flat or wherever else they decided to live. On granny's death mother had become the tenant of 92 and she had tasted independence. Granny had sown such suspicion of her husband in her mind that she would not accept him as tenant of 92 or anywhere else. I feel sure this must have been the cause of the breakdown; I remember my mother telling me that when my father left her soon after I was born she had sued him for maintenance towards my nurture but the magistrates had dismissed the case

Father in the work clothes of a market watchman in Sheffield in the 1930s. The market was probably the Rag Market off Commercial Street

because father had said he was willing to provide us with a home. So that was the end of that, but mother for some time tried to get information on what he was doing.

Father was at this time working as a watchman in the city markets and there was a man who lived in the top flat of the next passage in Campo Lane who had done similar work and kept in touch with the markets. I think my mother would really have liked to have rejoined my father but being proud and stubborn and having this burden of suspicion about him she contented herself by getting to know what he was doing. So that I suppose was why this elderly man from the next passage used to come round from time to time, sit on our horsehair sofa and blow clouds of evil-smelling smoke from his pipe; he smoked something called 'shag', which didn't smell like tobacco at all. He was a very inquisitive man, a man I disliked intensely, and I couldn't make out why my mother had him in the house. It was said that at night he would sit in his bedroom overlooking the street and watch everybody as they went up and down; he knew what time people went out and when they came back and whom they came back with. To achieve his object of knowing all there was to know about people, he sat in total darkness with the curtains drawn back and only the glow from his pipe breaking the blackness.

Lacking granny's pension mother was evidently finding difficulty making ends meet, for about this time she had to appeal to Public Assistance and we were allotted some grocery tokens for a while for her to get some basic foods from a designated shop. She used to go to an office near West Bar, in Corporation Street.

It was in the same area that I sometimes used to go to a cookshop for a basinful of meat and potato pie. There used to be several cookshops in our part of Sheffield. I seem to remember one in Cambridge Street; they were all like this one, which had a large window, partially obscured by steam. But in the middle of the window you could see the crust of a large pie, which was sunk in what I suppose was an oven; it used to smell and taste delicious.

Now what my mother had feared took place; our neighbours across the passage left us. Grace, Old Tom and Young Tom moved to a house in Oxford Street not far from Sheffield's first hospital, the Royal Infirmary, a street of Victorian houses which in those days were going down in the world. They invited us to visit them – this was in about 1925. Old Tom was working and Young Tom was upstairs with his teacher but we had tea with his mother and I remember we listened in wonder to the sounds coming from a thing like a gramophone horn fixed on the kitchen wall – 2LO, the latest triumph of science. The sound seemed strange and unreal but it was certainly louder and more comfortable to hear than the noises we had heard on a crystal set in Carlisle Street years before. There, when granny's nephew had the headphones on and was delicately moving the cat's whiskers on the crystal we had all to remain absolutely still; a cough or a sneeze was a terrible explosion of sound.

I have described how I stayed on at school in 1926 after I should have left because jobs were scarce in that year of strikes. But the time came when I could stay no longer and had to look for work; indeed I was desperately anxious to get work so as to be able to bring money home. The miners' strike was still continuing, with men still digging for coal on the spare ground next to the bus garage which had once been the Jungle, and jobs were hard to find, with scores, if not hundreds, of boys after every job. I remember little about the strikes which had such an effect on my job prospects. During the General Strike of 1926 there seemed a great quietness on the streets and I have one vivid picture of a procession of lorries passing me on the Wicker with the word 'Food' marked on their sides.

I have never been fervently religious, at least not to the extent of an outward show of piety and regular churchgoing. Yet the doctrines of the Church of England as expressed in my childhood during the six years or more I attended a church school have permeated my mind and influenced my thought and my conduct. If I could in any way be said to be a good man I owe it to the ideas that I received in those early days. Religion does give a sense of purpose to life, sometimes a sense of guidance which enabled me to accept whatever happened, although often there is that other thought that life is 'a tale told by an idiot . . . Signifying nothing.'

# CHAPTER TWELVE

# SEEKING WORK

In 1926, the year I left school and the year of strikes, the Labour Party won control of Sheffield, and they are still in charge. During the years immediately after 1926 the face of the districts around us began to change as the slums bit the dust and the slum-dwellers were banished to bleak, hygienic suburbs where possessing a bath compensated for life on cold, windy uplands.

Many employers used the method of selection used by a firm in Change Alley, a street no longer in existence. I arrived to find there were already boys queued up in front of me and more and more applicants formed up behind me. Then a man came into the street and walked along the line picking out the six tallest boys. Another memory is of a job on offer at the top of three flights of stairs at the Lloyds Bank building in Church Street where a line of boys stretched down the stairs and into the street. I soon realized that my small stature didn't improve my chances and I found my appearance was against me. I had black hair, a sallow skin and glasses. I found that some people thought I was a Jew. My headmaster, Mr Cowan, whom I think was a great man, had a name which when pronounced sounded like a common Jewish name, although it was spelt differently. I remember naming him to a prospective employer who looked at me as if he had seen a great light and said: 'He's a Jew, isn't he!'

My first job was in a pawnbrokers shop; they were still quite common at this time. There was one on the main shopping street, the Moor, and I think that was the one my mother used. My shop was in Porter Street at the back of the Moor. The man who owned it was one of a family of pawnbrokers. He was a nice man, 'straight', as people used to say. The shop itself was a grimy, shabby place that had not been painted for many years. Next door, and forming part of the business, was what I suppose had at one time been a house. All over Sheffield there were dirty, broken-down houses used as shops, workplaces and 'little mesters' quarters – this was one of them.

The first job in the morning and the last job at night was to carry large wooden shutters that covered the windows along a narrow passage to and from the back of the shop. These shutters were very thick and heavy and made of oak. It was as much as I could do to totter along with one of them on my shoulder. Inside the shop it was dark, with wide counters of wood and a couple of places like stalls for people to have privacy when they pawned their possessions. I had the job of pinning the pawn ticket on the pledge after it had been roughly parcelled, and take it to the store at the back of the shop where lines of shelves loaded with parcels rose to the roof, accessible by long heavy ladders. I soon discovered that the parcels were the habitation of fleas, but this did not worry me.

I was more worried by two other things in the shop; the thing that really frightened me was taking all sorts of heavy and bulky loads up to the floor above. The only access was by an almost vertical ladder. Having reached the upper floor you then had to carry out a rather delicate manoeuvre to get round a hole in the floor. The hole was in a glass skylight intended to light the shop below — evidently someone had fallen through the glass and it had never been repaired. The owner, as I have said, was a nice man — he was elderly and rather fat and kept exhorting himself with various business slogans, of which his favourite was 'Small Profits, Quick Returns'.

Starting work after school was something of a shock in the 1920s. In school you were cocooned against the world, here in my first job I was taken aback by the foul language and dirty stories that were part of life. I felt like a baby not understanding a lot that was said, or the sniggering and whispering that occurred, particularly when the owner was away and women came in with things to pawn and they and a couple of the men put their heads together muttering, laughing and shouting, 'That's a good 'un!' I don't suppose modern children have the same trouble.

One night when I got home my mother told me that the owner had been to see her to tell her that he was going to have to finish me. Although I was a good worker, he said he was afraid that I might have an accident falling off the ladder; that he could see I was frightened of heights. I was sorry to lose my first job when I was earning money for the first time. It was hard work; on Fridays and Saturdays we didn't finish until eight, but I had to admit that I felt fear at heights. Hard work didn't bother me.

So now it was back looking for work, writing letters and so on. The Unemployment Exchange in those days was in the red-brick, castellated Corn Exchange near the canal. As soon as you approached it you saw the long black line of men snaking round the walls and then you were part of the great mass of humanity slowly moving forward and exuding an air of hopelessness and despair. It might be cold and bleak outside but it was preferable to the hot, humid fug inside where the dingy walls seemed to sweat as streams of evil-looking moisture trickled slowly down. There was a continuous drone and hubbub of voices; harried, sweating clerks shouted at claimants and one another. This was a time when a father would have been able to direct me to the best and most likely way of getting a worthwhile job but I began to lose what little confidence I had and to feel that I couldn't do anything that people wanted.

One thing I had gained at school and which at one time buoyed my confidence was a certificate in an elaborate scarlet and gold cover. The Merit Certificate with distinction it said in History and Practical Science; this last was the product of what we had been taught in the laboratory. The lack of confidence I was beginning to feel caused me to look very unconvincing at interviews. I remember going for a clerk's job to a small steel firm where the manager, boss or whatever he was interviewed me with another man present, a friend I supposed. Fingering my certificate he said, 'History? Well, our own history's bad enough! What is an oxide?'

When he said that my mind seemed to freeze, I had no idea of the answer, it was as if I had never heard of the word. After a moment the interviewer turned to his companion and said: 'There you are! That's what modern schools do for you!'

At this time, 1927, I was sent to Bailey Street to something which I think was supposed to be a school for unemployed youth; it was held in St James's Church Rooms. I only went once to this place, which was full of lads. There was a man there who seemed to be a teacher, but nobody was paying any attention. It was impossible to make out what he was saying, even though he shouted from time to time, for there was continuous uproar from lads talking and shouting, some standing up, some sitting down on forms and banging with their hands and feet and throwing pellets of blotting paper.

I remember a little outing which my mother and I went on and I think it was the year after the General Strike. We were invited to tea at the house of the two sisters of the metallurgist who had his office in Figtree Lane. The two great strikes of 1926 affected a lot of people who were not directly involved, one of them being the metallurgist, whose office was cleaned by mother. His business was in a bad way and I don't think he could afford to pay for the cleaning she had carried out so his sisters came to the rescue to recompense mother in another way; she didn't blame their brother, she knew he would have paid her if he could. The thing I remember most clearly about the visit, which occurred on a warm sunny day, was the presence of two beautiful cats. They were Russian Blues and I don't think I've seen any since.

On Trippet Lane part of the building once occupied by Yorkshire Transport was now a Labour Exchange and a man from some agency took me to this place. I cannot recall what ensued but I did receive the strong impression that the officials there didn't like my conductor. Some while afterwards I remember this man being reported in the newspaper as being sentenced for offences against boys. Maybe it was the reason for the officials' coldness, but even after reading this report I thought nothing of it – I was a very innocent lad.

After a great many fruitless applications I did at length obtain another job. It was in an office block on Bank Street, or rather off Bank Street for you went through an entry into a courtyard surrounded by offices, one of which is now a night club. My employer had a stationery business on the top floor of a block; there was no lift and everything had to be carried up or down three flights of stairs. My function was to supply the transport for the business, wheeling large parcels of envelopes, writing paper, typing paper and suchlike all over Sheffield. To do this I was equipped with a metal barrow with long handles – a sack barrow I think it was called. Several times I had to wheel my load to factories in the East End, passing windows obscured by smoke and filth, through which one could see the red gleam of flames. This was of course a real dead-end job, but I was so desperate to earn money for my mother and had got such a poor opinion of myself that I stuck it until I was sacked. I think my fate was determined by a large bottle of ink which had been fastened on my sack barrow, but not fastened securely enough. When I pushed my barrow up the steep slope of Figtree Lane it broke loose, rolled off the barrow into the gutter and was shattered.

Time passed, I continued to chase jobs and I went to classes on shorthand and book-keeping, futile occupations for a male. Once when I went to Prestons, chemists and suppliers of laboratory equipment, the man whom I saw said: 'Learn a trade'. Wise words, but how was I to set about it? A father could have told me, but I had no father.

During some six years my prospects did not change but my surroundings did in human terms. The widow of the piano tuner died and the granddaughter, Mary, left and, we heard, married a librarian. The grocers shop across the road became a chip shop and we saw no more of the one-armed man and his wife. Our coalman retired and passed the business to his son-in-law, who tired of his wife and abandoned her and the business.

A little old lady who was a fervent Catholic came to live in the flat at the other side of our passage. She was a rather surprising person to live in our poverty-stricken district for both her sons were well-off; one owned a jewellers shop and the other was a partner in a firm of plumbers' merchants. The old lady was of a very independent nature. She was determined to live

School Lane off Duke Street, 1926

with neither of her sons but as near as possible to the two Catholic churches, St Marie's and St Vincent's, both near our flats. We had always been used to the sisters of Mercy going by in their white headdresses which, as a child, I called 'lard papers'. Our new neighbour explained that she had been a Protestant but had changed her religion for love of her husband. She would chuckle and say that when she was a young girl attending a private school they would pass the girls at a Catholic school and jeer at them, shouting: 'Catholic! Catholic! Ring the Bell. When you die you'll go to Hell,' and the Catholic girls would respond, 'Protestant! Protestant! Quack! Quack! Quack! Go to Old Harry and don't come back.' She was a very kind woman and loved playing the pop tunes of the moment on her piano. We could not help but be amused by her deadly rivalry with another old lady on matters like arranging stalls at Autumn and Christmas Fairs and placing the banners of the Women's Society in the right places.

Another lady who came to visit us when I was about 16 was a tall, gruff, middle-aged lady, said to be a colonel's daughter, who belonged to the Council for Social Service. I don't know whether she helped my mother, but I was called to her house to do some gardening. The house was a large, stone Victorian house in Collegiate Crescent where there are still many of them. I think the lady and her cook were the only inhabitants of the house. It had a big kitchen but it felt old-fashioned. However there was a lovely smell of cooking, particularly pastry made with a lot of fat. After a while I was taken outside and given a barrow and a besom, then the colonel's daughter showed me dead leaves, scattered about and in drifts. I was told to get them in piles, put them in the barrow and empty it at a certain place. I carried on doing this job until tea time but I had no idea why I was doing it – I thought it must be because she was a very tidy lady. Nobody in our district had gardens. I remember years later she called, when I had at length found a job, and she remarked: 'Ah! You have found a niche!' and I thought, 'Yes! I am above the floor but only just!'

This was the time when we had two Welsh ladies entitled 'Sisters' living in the flats who were in fact sisters in the flesh. The name 'Sister' had a religious significance not a medical one. One sister was attached to St James's and I am not sure where the other worked, but both wore dark-blue headdresses made of some flowing material that descended to their shoulders. They also wore coats and skirts of the same colour. Their duties seemed to be to help the parson and carry out visiting. The elder sister was a small gentle woman who used to talk about 'revivals' in the Welsh valleys and of the British being the lost ten tribes of Israel. She also told me encouragingly about a young man she knew who had become a missionary in Northern Canada and of his adventures in reaching Indians and Eskimos with his sledge. I was a very innocent, not to say pious, young man in those days and I felt that I could not possibly be good enough to be a minister. The old lady also told me of an uncle of hers called John who had been a trader in the Sudan at the time of General Gordon and how he had been killed in 1883 fighting with an army under General Hicks against the Dervishes. Her younger sister, Janey, was much taller but she was born with the handicap of having only one hand. She wore a dummy hand on which she put a glove and which gave her a normal appearance, but of course life was difficult for her and perhaps because of this she had a sharp tongue. They lived in a dark ground-floor flat at the end where Hawley Street flowed into Townhead Street.

During those years electricity was brought to the flats and almost everyone was delighted by the change. I say 'almost everyone' because the lady in the next passage who supervised the usherettes at the Albert Hall refused to have it installed. She was suspicious of electricity.

We still went to the Albert Hall which had now changed to talking pictures. Opposite it was a row of modest, undistinguished shops, one of which belonged to Cadman's the second-hand booksellers. I often stared in the windows at night but never ventured in. Very soon it was too late to go in – the shops disappeared to make way for the City Hall.

My mother went on going out cleaning and taking in washing; I did my best to help with the mangle and taking the washing back and forth. I used to take the parcels of washing to Pitsmoor and back. Sometimes I went to a family whose garden backed onto Burngreave Cemetery and the wife told me how during the influenza epidemic of 1919 they could see people with lanterns burying the dead by night as there were too many corpses to inter in daylight. These people had two things that interested me; one was a large, grey-and-blue parrot that climbed all over its cage and kept a sharp eye for anyone unwary enough to leave a finger within reach of its beak. The other interesting thing was a lodger, a male teacher. This man was very kind when he saw me and used to give me copies of the *Teachers' World* whose book reviews interested me. Here, in articles on book-collecting, I came upon a very strange notion – that books were more valuable if the pages had not been cut. The lady with the parrot had a daughter who was married to the son of a commander in the City Fire Brigade. My mother cleaned at the fire chief's flat for a long time, for I was only a small boy at first and I remember a fireman called Charlie sitting me on the front seat of a fire engine, for long a source of pride to me. My mother used to be given copies of a large-size magazine called *Nash's* which was about the size of the present *Country Life*. Unlike *Country Life* its large photos were of actors and actresses in West End shows but there were also serials by A.E.W. Mason,

Robert Hichens, and Somerset Maugham, and also short stories by Maugham. How I enjoyed those stories, mainly set in Malaya ('Footprints in the Jungle', 'The Out Station', etc.) and Capri.

There was a bookshop in Charles Street facing the Empire Theatre which was closing down at this time. Looking wistfully at the books in the window I was astonished to see a leather-bound copy of the *Poems* of Thomas Moore for 1s 9d, a sum I could just scrape together. When I went in the shop, the departing owner looked at the book in amazement. 'It's been marked up wrong,' he said. 'It should have been four and sixpence!' but I got it.

Broad Lane, quite near to us, was another place that would change its residential character – its pawnshop would become just another shop and most of the other shops would wither away. One of them for years was a grocer's, only a small shop, really the front room of a house but bursting with provisions. You stepped straight off the pavement into a dark room like a cellar, always liable to be flooded in heavy rains. At midday, hot soup was sold by the shop; and I think sandwiches, in fact anything to make money. The couple who owned the shop were a contrast. The wife was a stolid, hard-working woman who was mostly behind the scenes. The husband was the business brain, the man in the shop. He was slim, dark and elegant – someone who could have passed for a doctor or a professor – and sometimes when business was slack he would tell me of concerts he had been to. One in particular remains in my memory, when he told me he had been to hear 'Rack-man-in-off' play the piano. No doubt he foresaw the changes in the district and when his wife died he soon departed. I often wondered what happened to him; with his long, thin, delicate fingers, his calm, polite manner and well-cared-for hair he would have fitted into societies far different from the slums of Sheffield.

# CHAPTER THIRTEEN

# LIFE AT LAYCOCKS

At long last I gained a job. It was at a firm in the Millhouses district, an area of middle-class owner-occupiers, parks, and substantial pubs. The firm I was to work for during the next twenty years or more had come back from the dead, rescued and given artificial respiration by T.W. Ward, then Sheffield's leading company doctor. Its prosperity in the past, as a supplier of equipment to British and overseas railway systems, was attested by a large and impressive office building and a wide spread of workshops. Work for the railways still formed a part of current output, albeit a declining part. The motor industry and re-armament were the sources of the factory's new prosperity. In our stamp shop a lot of the work consisted of flanges for the propeller shafts of cars and lorries, crankshafts and parts for garage equipment; parts for the production of vehicles or parts for hoists, jacks, carwashers, etc.

As we wage-earners trudged down a steep slope into the works yard, we could see to our right a large boilerhouse with a lofty chimney and then a continuous block of buildings, machine shops and fitting shops. There was also a great expanse of empty yard broken only by a dilapidated, single-storey tin building, the Heat Treatment, where there were a couple of gas furnaces, tanks of whale oil, cyanide boxes and an oppressive sultry atmosphere where the chirping of crickets never ceased as they shot from place to place like bullets.

I was to work in the Forge, a term which covered blacksmiths, dropstampers and die sinkers. Reaching the bottom of the drive and turning left for the Forge I could see beyond it the Buffing Shop, the Railway Shop, the Foundry, the Fettlers, the Sheet Metal Shop, the Joiners, the Plating Shop and behind them all the Steel Stores and, closing the vision, the railway line with trains flashing past. This part of the yard was built up; here there was no room for expansion. It was on the other side that new developments would take place.

Conditions in the Forge were unpleasant for everybody. The shop was dark, the only natural light was from skylights in the roof and from outside when the sliding doors to the yard were pushed back. A third of the space was filled by the blacksmiths, their hearths, anvils and water tanks or 'boshes' in which they quenched the steel.

The drop forge occupied two-thirds of the shop. A line of coke furnaces stood opposite a line of drop hammers and shapers; each drop hammer had one die mounted in the base and another in the top and the product was shaped by the repeated blows of the hammer. (Although in those days before the advent of the machine saws a rough shaping process would take place on the shaper.) At the back of the hammers was a line of presses where the surplus metal round the stampings was sheared off. When the hammer struck the orange red steel for the first time it sounded almost like butter being struck.

When I arrived, stamping was being carried out straight from the bar, the bar of steel being brought out of the furnace body in a pair of tongs to be rough-shaped on the shaper. It was then put back in the furnace to be reheated for the stamping operation. The stamper would be pouring out floods of sweat at this time and if he came in the office any paper would be covered in droplets of sweat.

Not having had a proper job for so long, I felt a sense of release and of pleasure to be doing things. I thought of the words of William Blake, 'Energy is eternal delight.' Perhaps it was as well that I felt like this for my wage was very small. In my earliest days at the job my office, which I shared with the foreman, was a little wooden hutch just inside the shop, behind one of the sliding doors and up three steps. As the hammers rose and fell, the whole structure shuddered and trembled. I remember on my first or second day I had to send for one of the stampers and he came bouncing into the office, sweat streaming from him like water. I had never seen anyone sweat like that before. The sweat poured off his head, face, hands, everywhere. He made a little puddle on the floor and the paper I wanted to show him was blotted and wetted in a second.

'Are you Mr H?' I said.

'Yes sir! Yes sir! Three bags full!' he replied.

The blacksmiths' fires burned a small specialized type of coke called breeze. The skilled blacksmith could adjust the heat of his hearth over a wide range of temperatures to suit the product he was making or hardening. The coke fires used by the dropstampers used a coarser kind of coke and needed replenishing every couple of hours. This was a very unpleasant few minutes, for there were great clouds of sour smelling sulphurous smoke

Laycocks' works in Archer Road, Millhouses, seen from the air, *c.* 1935

drifting everywhere until the fuel burnt through, penetrating everything, getting in eyes, noses and mouths.

When I started working in the Forge I soon discovered that there was ill feeling in the shop. A little while before I arrived the foreman in charge had retired. He was an old and experienced man, well respected by the workers. Because his name was that of a pork product and because he was a man of few words who grunted more often than he spoke he was called 'Piggy'. Piggy had been succeeded by George, a deeply unpopular man who was a die sinker. He tried to get the stampers to reveal the secrets of their trade. Once he had learned these, they said, he tried to use his new knowledge against them. In consequence they had ceased to co-operate with him but simply obeyed orders, even when they knew the outcome would be failure.

As a newcomer who had never seen a dropstamp before, it took me a little while to understand the situation. I could see there was something wrong when George got one of the stampers to get a bar of 3 inch square steel nearly white hot in a coke furnace, then holding the cool end in a pair of tongs with the weight being taken by a pulley, he directed the stamper to take it to a shaping hammer and shape it to his instructions. The bar was turned over from side to side but it was obvious something was wrong, the shape wasn't right. The bar was cooling rapidly, scale was forming and the bar had to be put back into the furnace. The other stampers came up, grinning; any one of them could have put things right or said how it could be done but they weren't going to rescue George. George meanwhile stood by with a smile on his face as if he knew what he was doing. Again the bar was brought out of the furnace and again it was no good. I can't remember what happened, perhaps the metal had to be wasted.

The men talked nostalgically of Piggy and wished he were back. Piggy had also had his problems, as when he had once set on a giant blacksmith from Northumberland who after a couple of days wanted to leave.

'You'll have to work your week out,' said Piggy.

The Geordie gripped the foreman by the throat and held him against the wall.

'Ah want ma bawbees!' he said – and he got them.

My job in the Forge was to free the foreman from clerical work and provide the documentation from which the Wages Office could work out wages and the Cost Office could discover the production cost of every job. To achieve these objectives I had to fill in job cards and clock them at the time a job started, clock off when one job was finished and clock onto another job card for the next job. The clocking was accomplished by pushing the card into an orifice on the side of a clock that rested on a table immediately below a window in the glass wall of the office. Various particulars had to be written on the job card before it was clocked, such as the name of the worker, his check numbers, the internal order number of the job, the part number and quantity of the parts to be done, and the price in money or time of the individual part. When the job was finished I had to work out and enter on the job card the number of hours and minutes taken and the quantities passed by inspection. Every Monday morning I would collect the job cards and check that the hours on the cards agreed with actual hours worked as shown on the operator's time card. Among the particulars entered on the job card in the case of blacksmiths or dropforgers would be the name and number of their respective partners: the blacksmith's striker and the dropstamper's driver. When orders were scarce, men would be on 'day work', the basic rate, but when piecework was in operation the proceeds would be divided between the partners as follows: the blacksmith or dropstamper would get 49/63 (or 7/9) of the money earned; the rest would go to the striker or hammer driver.

It was my responsibility to point out to the foreman those jobs which had not paid and also where the profit earned seemed out of proportion. I had to have the quantities checked, arrange for them to be moved elsewhere in the factory, procure raw materials from the steel stores for production and if we began to run short of work go to the Progress Office and check with each progress man to see if he had orders which he had not yet put out.

On pay day I would take any complaints or queries to the Wages Office on the top floor of the office block, which in the early days of financial stringency involved walking up three flights of stone steps. Apart from the blacksmiths, strikers, dropstampers and hammer drivers there were the trimmers, whose job was to take the hot stampings in a pair of tongs to the trimming press to have the surplus material or 'fash' removed. In the early days of coke furnaces there were two youngsters who brought barrowloads of coke in from the yard. Finally, there were the die sinkers, who produced the impressions on steel dies from which the products were fashioned under the drop hammers (these regarded themselves with some justice as an elite) and there were the odd two or three machinists who operated the milling, turning and planing machines in the same department.

Despite the noise, the heat and the smells I enjoyed my new job, totting up hours of work and quantities produced, getting raw material from the steel stores, and liaising with the Progress Office, the Buying Office and the Wages Office.

At length the unpopular foreman, George, left. He said to me, 'Syd [the works manager] wants me to do more work wi'out more pay. I'm not having that. I expect he'll get Maurice to take over.'

His successor was indeed Maurice, one of the blacksmiths, a master of his craft and a man who understood dropforging. Usually a calm man, he was subject to fits of frustration and depression when he would suddenly throw down his work, curse, throw his tools in all directions and walk out of the shop. On one occasion his striker, who was getting sick of this sort of performance, watched the hammer, tongs and pincers go flying down the shop, rushed to the anvil, put his arms round it and called: 'Gie me a hand!'

'What's up wi' thee?' Maurice growled.

'We're working outside, aren't wi'?' said the striker.

Soon after Maurice took charge the dropstampers' coke furnaces were replaced by gas. The new gas furnaces were installed under the direction of Jack, a dark-haired young man who had just come back from Cornwall where he had been doing similar work and where he said the locals were all asleep. Thick ropes for the drop hammers were now kept in quantity and an ex-Royal Navy sailor called Albert was set on to splice ropes. According to his own account, Albert had been dismissed from the Navy for his part in the Invergordon mutiny in 1931. For a time, Albert was also storekeeper in the Steel Stores, a lofty, hangar-like building close to the railway line.

The stamper, Bill, as everyone called him, whom I had called into the office on my first or second day, was an enormously strong man who had been a professional footballer playing for three League clubs before hanging up his boots. He still kept in training, but now his sport was cricket and after a while he changed to being an umpire.

His closest friend, Billy, was one of the blacksmiths, a dark-haired man in his early 30s, who was without doubt the noblest man I have ever known. He was one of those men who will wear themselves out trying to help other people. As shop steward he spent many, many hours arguing and negotiating for the benefit of other people – hours and hours in which he could have earned himself money. But working for the union and his workmates was only a part of the story. If he saw anyone in need of help he was compelled by his nature to intervene on their behalf. He looked after everybody's interests but his own. Above all he was a man with such a sense of justice and fair play that he would never invoke any argument or indulge in any practice that savoured of deceit. Billy had a lot of talent, he was a good mathematician who could work out the most intricate cash and arithmetical arrangements, a beautiful handwriter, an accomplished sketcher and campanologist; he lacked only one thing – luck.

He had ill fortune throughout his life. His father died when he was at school where he showed such promise that his headmaster besought his mother not to take him away before his fourteenth year. The headmaster came to see the mother to plead with her to keep the boy at school and give him a better chance of a decent job, but it was in vain. All the mother cared about was the few shillings Billy could bring home. She had married again and she and her new husband pushed the sensitive child into a dead-end job: plucking poultry as soon as their necks were wrung and when they were still warm, quivering, barely dead.

As soon as he was old enough the youth joined the army on the Western Front, where he was badly wounded. On his return to civvy street he got a job as a blacksmith's striker and supplemented his wage by teaching dancing – he also fell in love. Falling in love with Kitty was another stroke of ill fortune. Not until after they were married did he learn something her family had concealed from him – that there was a streak of insanity in the family. Her brother had died in an asylum. Although Billy seemed cheerful and relaxed, as I learned later his wife had already spent a period in a mental hospital and worse times lay ahead. Throughout the fifty years of the marriage she suffered periods of mental instability, leading to confinement in mental hospitals. He was a man who remained faithful to his wife 'in sickness and in health' but though fond of children he felt it would not be right to bring children into the world affected by the same handicap that darkened his and Kitty's lives.

In the Forge as elsewhere most of the middle-aged men had fought in the Great War and had no desire to see another. Many of them respected the Germans as soldiers and wished they had been on our side and thought they had been badly treated at the Treaty of Versailles. Men like 'Yanks', who was ex-Machine Gun Corps, could laugh and joke about most things except being sent to attack enemy trenches through clinging mud where the Germans had put red rags on gaps in the barbed wire.

'We ses to our captain! "We can't get through that lot! It's bloody murder!" and he says: "Them's the orders!"'

Another man I used to talk to, Ernest, the first aid man, had been a stretcher bearer all through the War. Now he was in charge of the drawing stores: racks and racks of blueprints pasted on boards. I frequently went for drawings and always enjoyed his salty Rabelaisian conversation in which politicians, women and some of our fellow workers were held up to derision. The war had given Ernest a taste for the Continent and he went there for his holidays every year, although he didn't seem to have a very high opinion of the French. He said: 'They're quick-tempered buggers. If you're in a dance hall there, it only takes a little thing to set them off and in no time they're chucking chairs through the windows.' One thing he did approve of was the gas jets that burned in *estaminets* for the patrons to light their cigarettes at.

In the Forge, following the change from coke furnaces to gas furnaces, the next step was the arrival of sawing machines which cut pieces of steel called 'users' off the bars. Each piece of steel was supposed to be of a weight and size to make one stamping, but in the case of a new stamping, a new design, the size of the user had to be arrived at by a process of trial and error. The sawing machines had been made in Germany and staff from the makers, Heller, came to instal them and explain their operation to those men who were going to use them. This led to a ticklish situation, for at the end of our shop a communicating door led to a shop which under the Government's Shadow Re-armament programme had been designated as a Shell Shop where brand-new machinery had been installed for turning shells. Strict instructions were given that the door was to be kept locked all the time the German engineers were present but I expect they knew all about our secret.

Billy the blacksmith and I used to go home on the same tram and get off at what was then called Coles Corner, opposite Boots and facing the cathedral, after which he had to catch another tram to get to the heights of Walkley. One evening in 1936 after jumping off the tram we saw on the newsvendor's placard the words 'Civil War in Spain'; at the time it didn't seem very important.

At this time after I had eaten my sandwiches I would spend the rest of the lunch hour in the Progress Office, which was just across the yard. At first it was on the ground floor with the drawing office on the floor above. Before a canteen came into existence most of the lads who stayed there to eat their 'snap' talked about the ever popular subject of girls, but later on when most went to the canteen I used to talk to a young Progress man called John, who was an all-round musician. He played the piano and organ, and was studying conducting. He did me a great service by introducing me to music in those lunch breaks.

There was another youth, a new recruit to the Progress Office. He was a trumpet player who played in a jazz band. My friend John induced him to bring his trumpet to work with a view to some joint practice, he beating time and Jack trumpeting with me and a fat, disagreeable youth from the machine shop as audience. Jack was not able to do himself justice as he was nervous in case the works manager, Syd, might be in his office nearby, so this first practice was also the last. Soon afterwards Jack read that the band leader and trumpeter Roy Fox had contracted tuberculosis and immediately abandoned the trumpet and took up the saxophone. He never brought his new instrument to practise as he was too terrified of Syd to risk it. He was not alone. Most people found the manager a rather alarming person. Syd was a short, fat man who had such a dominant personality that a single word or his mere presence was enough to send people scurrying in all directions. I remember years later a foreman who always took his false teeth out to eat his lunch in his little office. He was doing this at lunchtime one day when an operator knocked on the window and said: 'Syd's in the shop!' 'Eh? What!' the foreman said, then grabbing his teeth he dashed in search of Syd, stuffing the teeth in his mouth as he went. It was an occasion of great but concealed mirth among the workers.

During the years immediately before the Second World War, a series of changes took place – new markets, more employees and an increase in the size of the factory. For instance, a new department came into existence known as the Scratching Shop where men worked with files deburring aircraft components made in Duralumin, a light, shiny metallic material new to us. A firm of professional caterers were employed to set up a new Works Canteen, which replaced a modest enterprise operated by the daughter of a man in the Tool Room.

Work and jobs continued to increase as we left the middle 1930s behind and the word 'war' once more surfaced. Uniformed gatemen appeared at the top of the drive, checking movements in and out. They were under the command of a retired police sergeant and after a while everyone had a pass with a passport-sized photograph to establish their identity.

A lady personnel officer arrived and opened an office, a sign that someone foresaw that if war came it would bring in many more workers, including women, and that someone would be needed possessing patience and tact to listen to people's grievances and take the heat out of situations. The new personnel officer had earned her living as a professional writer and in the future was to prove a great success.

There was much concern expressed in the papers about the low level of physical fitness in the country and firms were urged to set up schemes for exercises, athletics, etc. At our firm, the company secretary, himself a keep-fit enthusiast, was charged with the task of getting the workers involved in exercises, running, etc. I declined an invitation to join as I disliked organized keep-fit schemes and I had noticed that many of those who devoted most time to sport and physical exercise didn't seem to be any healthier. Our own organizer was a case in point. He died still young. In those days there were no Government warnings: 'Physical exercise may endanger your health'!

Our world had now become a switchback bound to end in war, but the end of the Munich crisis seemed at the time a miraculous deliverance. The few in the factory who thought we should have fought while the enemy had not reached full strength were called 'warmongers'. I was one of them.

# CHAPTER FOURTEEN

# PRELUDE TO WAR

Now let us see what had been happening in the flats during the six years before the Second World War, a time when there was marked change both in the little community and in that part of Sheffield that surrounded us. In our passage all the flats except ours changed hands.

Miss Minnie, who lived with her mother in the larger of the two top flats, went to Switzerland on holiday and while she was away her mother was found dead. Having settled her mother's affairs, Minnie put into action what she had long meditated. She took early retirement from the bank and was accepted as a missionary, but for Jamaica, not for India as she had hoped; there were no vacancies in India. The death of Minnie's mother brought an answer to a problem that had long puzzled the other occupants of the passage: who was the elderly upright man who came up the stairs every Sunday at teatime and departed two hours later? He turned out to be the old lady's second husband.

Miss Sally, who lived in the smaller of the two top flats, had retired from Coles and apart from the weekly meeting of the Plymouth Brethren, a small amount of shopping, visits to her brother and one or two friends, she seldom ventured downstairs and one felt she did not welcome visits from her neighbours. After climbing three flights of stairs one had to declare oneself and wait while locks were unfastened and a chain removed. It was with surprise, therefore, that we began to receive unexpected visits from Miss Sally. She would enter clutching a large bunch of keys which she kept rattling nervously. She seemed to have come down without purpose and having arrived was anxious to get back to her lonely flat. It was a sign of a mental disorder which led her, the most modest of women, to come downstairs in her nightdress seeking refuge from whatever demon was tormenting her. Death was not long in ending her misery.

In the flat above us the dressmakers had been succeeded by a widow with three teenage children. Not long after they arrived, King George V died. At this time we did not possess a radio but our new neighbours invited us up to listen to the broadcast taking place while the king's life was ebbing away. There were a number of deaths among people we knew during those few years. Our new neighbour above had only a little time left when she invited us up to listen to her radio.

The Catholic family who lived in the top flat of the next passage lost their eldest boy and not long afterwards his mother. In those days the flats were like a big village and a death was a matter of concern to everyone. First there would be hurried footsteps and whispering as the wise women who laid out the dead would be sent for and then in the days before the funeral a group of women neighbours would go from flat to flat, up and down stairs, collecting money for a wreath. However little money she had, mother would always give them something. At the same time as one was asked for a contribution there would be an invitation: 'Do you want to see him?' but sometimes it would be: 'She's not going to keep so they've had to screw her up!' I was very impressed when I was told that Francis the Catholic boy would have candles round his coffin. 'That's what they do, Catholics,' people said. 'Put candles round the coffin.' Francis was not a friend of mine but I did feel interested because years before when I was at school I was ambushed on Leopold Street by a gang of lads who beat me and broke my spectacles, under the impression that I was Francis.

Coming back to changes in our passage, we were very sorry when the little old Catholic lady next to us announced that she had yielded to the entreaties of her family and was going to live somewhere nearer to them and quieter.

After her came another strong-minded old lady who I think had worked in cutlery and was a very unsociable person. She had a family who had all got on in the world and objected to her living in the flats. She was illiterate, and when letters came she just threw them on the fire back. These letters not only included bills and tax demands but correspondence from well-to-do offspring enclosing bank notes. All went on the fire. One day the old lady surprised us by coming into our flat and saying to my mother: 'Look! I don't want you to do owt for mi! If my folks ask you, say that you come and see me every day! I'm not leaving here to suit them!' Not long afterwards death solved her problem and took her away.

She was followed by a blind couple, both elderly. The husband was partly sighted, but this advantage was offset by his being almost stone deaf. This resulted in his neighbours hearing all the couple's domestic conversation, and also their radio was always turned up so high that it was audible all over the passage and in the street. The old gentleman was devoted to his wife and when she became ill he was distraught. I can't remember what happened but they left.

The next tenants were a couple of elderly Irish sisters. One had been married, the other was a spinster. Both had poor eyesight and they could not see specks of dirt, food and dust that dropped on the floor and the furniture and floated in the air to attach themselves to walls. They lived across the passage from us for more than twenty years so that at the end both the eye and the nose were assailed. The old ladies were passionately fond of cats, and feline friends shared everything they had, before, during and after the War. Like most cats they loved high places. They sat on the table, the piano and the mantelpiece and were pampered with the best of everything but were never let out of the flat.

We too had cats for about twenty years. They were mother and daughter. The mother was a highly intelligent black-and-white, the terror of all dogs that ventured near us. At the due time she was courted by three or four

Mother with the cat 'Spud' in about 1950. The flats are in the background

toms, who placed themselves in strategic positions round our front steps, making a hideous noise with much hissing and spitting that erupted at times into fights. Her daughter was left on our hands because the girl from Carlisle Street asked us to save a kitten for her and then her miner brother who lived with her bought a canary. The kitten was smaller than its mother when adult and a browny-ginger colour. Both cats used to like to sharpen their nails on our big table, standing at full stretch to reach one corner. The younger cat used to love to haul herself upright on the fireguard, warming her chest, and sometimes climbed onto the top and balanced uncomfortably while she stared into the fire. Both cats died before the war, so feeding them in the times of shortage and rationing was one worry we did not have.

All this time my mother was suffering from the ulcers on her legs which had broken out after the accident in which her hands had been trapped by the sash window when its cord broke, in the office in Figtree Lane. At first only one leg was affected but after a while both legs had ulcers that were discharging. At the end of every evening the old bandages had to be taken off and replaced by fresh ones. Sometimes the bandages had become stuck in the discharge and I had to bathe them as gently as I could, first to release the old bandage and then to prepare for the fresh bandage. The holes that the ulcers had made never really dried up, but they were worse sometimes than others. This was the background to life for some twenty-five years.

There was a change in our milk supplies. My childhood friend who wore leggings and had a horse float sold the business to a man from Oughtibridge who was a nice man but much more laconic. He it was who changed over from a horse float to a motor van and from pouring milk into a basin to leaving bottles.

When the grocer's shop in Campo Lane became a fish-and-chip shop we started getting our groceries from a corner shop at the bottom of Townhead Street. It was half-moon shaped and from its doorway you had a good view of the tower of St Vincent's church. The shop was run by a Catholic lady in late middle age. The thing I remember about the shop in her time was a very large tabby cat that sat on the counter quite contentedly purring loudly in a throaty voice.

On the Campo Lane side of our passage was a further passage and then running up to the iron gates there was a flat consisting of a single room. An unemployed man lived there and I remember his wife, a woman who was very thin and very pale with a face like paper. I had noticed that the lower part of her body was getting fat but I was astonished to hear some women talking about her. 'She ought to stop inside.' 'It's disgusting! It's fairly sitting on her!' I didn't know what they were talking about.

My friend Tommy had gone and Charlie, Miss Minnie's nephew, had gone to London. So for a while I had no friends. Then Albert and his parents came into the ground-floor flat of the Campo Lane passage. Albert's father had a well-paid job in the cutlery industry; they seemed nice people and Albert and I used to get on a tram to Fulwood and other pleasant districts of Sheffield and walk and explore what seemed the endless variety of the city. Albert's mother confided in my mother that her husband was very jealous and always wanted to know where she went. One day the two mothers decided to go to Chatsworth to picnic in the park. As we walked along Leopold Street, Albert's mother pointed out her husband shadowing us from the other side of the road but a long way behind.

'There!' she said, 'I told you how jealous he is!'

We were much impressed. I don't know how much time elapsed, but one night the husband came home from work, handed the housekeeping money over and said: 'That's it! I'm leaving you! But I'll bring you this money every week.' And so he did. On the same night every week he would enter the flat, put the money on the table, and leave without a word being said on either side. This arrangement lasted for years.

The two Welsh sisters who were church workers had left the flats on the elder sister's retirement. They had gone to live in a house on Sheaf Gardens Terrace. It was a small house with a minute garden in a terrace where every two houses shared a courtyard. At the time the fact that the street was near a railway goods yard didn't seem to matter. I used to go and see the sisters from time to time. They both seemed happy in their new surroundings. The elder sister was one of those gentle people who look at the world through rose-coloured spectacles. She liked to sit on the easy chair, whose brass plate said it was a gift from the parishioners, and nurse her large tabby cat Catherine, who despite the name was a tom given to nocturnal expeditions over the rooftops. Nursing the cat my Welsh friend would talk about the British Israelites and whether one should take notice of the prophecies of the Great Pyramid; of one thing she was certain, the battle of Armageddon was approaching.

Political meetings seemed to have died out but in compensation we got more religious meetings, mainly led by the Salvation Army. It was usually a silver band that assembled in the yard although sometimes there would be concertinas and tambourines. The music was what made people come to their doors and stand at the end of their balconies. One of the 'Sallies' would shout out the words of the hymn before the band burst out. Then one would see other men and women rushing up and down stairs with collecting bags. Very few people refused to give a few coins. The service over, they would break up and go through the passages to Townhead Street where they would re-form behind their flag. As they stepped off up the hill a little man used to run ahead shouting something, of which the only words you could hear were 'Salvation Army'. All was silent except the sombre beat of the bass drum. It was said that the band remained silent out of respect for St James's church and its vicar, Mr Parsons. As soon as they had crossed the tramlines into Leopold Street, there would be a double beat on the drum and the band would begin a lively tune that would take them to the Citadel in Lower Burgess Street.

Apart from the changes in the flats, changes took place around us in those years between my getting a regular job and the outbreak of war.

St James's church rising behind the Golden Ball seemed the embodiment of permanency; under Dawson Parsons it seemed more prosperous than it had been for decades. Every year in autumn the Police Band would come to play at the Harvest Festival. The Chief Constable himself would be there; it was Major James, the successor to gang-buster Percy Sillitoe, and it all meant that one Sunday at least the church would be full.

The row of stone houses on Campo Lane just beyond the Golden Ball was demolished but before the buildings disappeared a curious incident took

Pinstone Street, Sheffield, in the 1920s. St Pauls, on the right, was demolished c. 1935 and replaced with the Peace Gardens

place. There was a lady living in one of the houses who was a toper – one who was often merry but never incapable. On this particular day the Salvation Army had made a call at the flats and for some reason had held a short service outside our passage. Among the audience was the lady from across the way. Suddenly she thrust forward and knelt at the feet of the speaker, proclaiming her sinfulness and her desire to repent. The speaker, startled, raised her up and she left with them as they set off for the Citadel. The conversion was lasting. She was never the worse for alcohol again – in fact, she gave up drink altogether.

Buildings changed their use or disappeared and now I can't remember when such and such an event occurred. For example, when the coal-black Shambles were replaced by the C&A building, or when what seemed to us in our poverty to be enormously posh restaurants and shops like the Bodega in High Street, Tuckwoods and the Winchester café on Fargate vanished. I remember the sumptuous smell of coffee from the Winchester. Then, only the toffs drank coffee.

One well-loved building vanished in a spectacular blaze in 1934. We were in the great crowd of people who watched the Albert Hall burn down. One of the last films my mother and I saw there was a spy drama set in Soviet Russia called *Forbidden Territory*. The last manager of the Albert Hall was a Mr Deacon and the cinema company found him another job in London. A few years later we heard that this poor fellow and his wife had been killed in the London Blitz.

Not long before the Albert Hall met its end a young man came from Northern Ireland to learn the business of being a cinema manager, but after a short time he returned to where his family were involved in the linen business. With true Irish generosity he left behind a present for everyone, including me whom he had never met. His name was Mr Montgomery and I thought I should never hear the name again.

Both our synagogues were no longer used for worship and their replacement by a new synagogue at Wilson Road, Ecclesall, meant the end of a sight which always impressed me. On Sunday mornings bearded men clad in black, wearing wide-brimmed black hats, would walk past the Golden Ball and step out towards Leopold Street. These 'Rabbis', as we called them, were usually in earnest conversation with middle-aged soberly dressed business types and walking respectfully behind them would be a number of boys and youths silently and modestly following their elders.

Two unsuccessful ventures opened and closed in Campo Lane. A fruit and vegetable shop called The Dugout opened in part of what had been the coalyard and after they closed another greengrocers opened in a little shop adjoining the entrance to the Hawley Street flats. The locals speculated that this last shop had been opened by people who had won money on the pools. The football pools were just beginning to be known and in the windows of bookshops like Hartley Seeds on Church Street a mysterious book by one R.J. Russell appeared called *The Peril of the Pools*. I was sorry when this second shop closed, for a very pretty girl was in charge of it – I found a great attraction in the oranges she had for sale but I was too tongue-tied to advance any further beyond making purchases.

At the other end of the flats, where the kosher butcher had operated the shop at the top of Silver Street, nobody succeeded him for decade after decade.

At the Golden Ball there was a change of licensee. The new landlord had been something at the Grand Hotel. He was a distinguished-looking man with a moustache, and had a wife, son and daughter. I was more interested in his animal family. This consisted of a beautiful red setter, a large and dignified black cat, and a small black-and-white fox terrier. It was very amusing in the early days to see these three animals set out together for a walk. The black cat went first, then came the terrier. The red setter – impatient at the slow progress – galloped round and round the other two. The three seemed to be very good friends. I think the landlord must have found the Golden Ball a sad place. Two of his three animal friends died: the fox terrier was knocked down, the cat was perhaps poisoned. And then his wife died. The red setter spent most of its time lying in the doorway of the Best Room on Townhead Street but its moment came at closing time when it gave a series of ear-splitting barks as he took it out last thing at night.

An old friend came to help at the Ball – it was Old Tom. It seemed to be a job that suited him. My mother had come across him some years before in the Cathedral Yard at Whitsuntide. It had been a melancholy occasion. People spoke sadly of the great gatherings that had taken place in years gone by, of how even the meetings of the Chapel choirs and scholars in the parks were diminishing, and the old tradition of children getting new clothes for Whitsun and going round relatives and friends showing them off was dying. The bands of choristers and Sunday School scholars from St James's and other neighbouring churches seemed shrunken in numbers. Old Tom had been in a depressed mood. Yes! Young Tom was all right and doing well, his benefactor had taken him to London to meet some of his family. He remarked gloomily that he had lost a lot of his faith in the Labour Party. For years he had spent a lot of his time working for Labour in Sheffield, addressing envelopes for hours and hours. Now he felt there wasn't all that much difference between Labour politicians and any other sort. He seemed thoroughly disillusioned.

When this period of my life started we used to take the weekly paper *John Bull* and I particularly remember an article called 'Europe's Private Armies', which I think must have been early in 1930, in which the author listed sundry organizations all over Europe such as the *Stahlhelm*, the *Heimwehr*, the *Croix de Feu* and several other groups, including a very brief paragraph which said something like 'and round Munich there are the Hitlerites'. Somehow at the time it seemed exciting rather than menacing; everywhere the conventional politicians – corrupt and helpless – seemed unable to get anything done.

It was not only the decline of the Whitsun Sing that gave us the feeling of things running down. My barber on West Bar died and from that day to this I never seem to have felt the same about any of the barbers I have tried. Our doctor died as well. He was a large man who seemed to fill his chair and exude confidence and a sort of massive certainty in what he said. His successor was a young Scotsman from Edinburgh, I think, and the reason I thought so was that he got all the stamps he collected free from foreign sailors at Leith.

The British Legion departed and the Sheffield Playhouse came into the same quarters at the bottom of Little Hill, fronting Townhead Street. It was not often that mother and I could afford to go and I think someone gave me a ticket to see my first play there, which was *The Imaginary Invalid* by Molière. It was very seldom that we went to the theatre but looking back now one realizes what a wonderfully high standard was maintained for years, with a fresh play every fortnight. One play which really thrilled me was *Macbeth* in which there had been a last-minute change in the cast due to illness. An actor I had never heard of called Alec Guinness played the title role and I shall never forget the tension, the absolute silence, as Macbeth crept stealthily to Duncan's chamber. Sitting in the Playhouse on an evening like that who could have imagined that gimmicks and gadgets would one day take over.

A change for the better was the completion of the new Central Library. Elsewhere, in the roads, parks and sports grounds men began pedalling dark-blue tricycles on which were inscribed the words, 'Stop Me and Buy One!'; it was the beginning of the end for the traditional wooden ice-cream barrow.

All the time in the decade before the Second War the face of Sheffield was changing, but we in the flats were not troubled by the demolition of old housing and the transfer of people to the new estates – in fact we hardly noticed it. It was only when I went to my doctor's surgery on Meadow Street that I began to notice a strange silence, and the time I remember walking just for pleasure past Queen's Tower and climbing up a long hill and coming on great scars and wounds on the land where hordes of men were starting to build a new estate. It was during this period that my old school, the Cathedral school in Queen Street, was finally closed. The headmaster then was the man who had read *Treasure Island* to us and opened our eyes to Shakespeare's plays.

# CHAPTER FIFTEEN

# SURVIVAL 1939–40

In September 1939 the war which had been expected and feared at last broke out. Events turned out very differently to expectations. There was no cataclysm. The shattering blows from the sky which would destroy civilization and, it was predicted, would turn us into a ragged mob living in ruined cities, did not occur. Instead we had the blackout, which almost brought life to a standstill after dark. It was as if we had been blinded – wire netting covered the windows of trams and buses with only tiny peepholes to see where you were, and that was little use at night. Coming from work I would, like everyone else, grope my way slowly and uncertainly to the flats, stopping at the pavement edge and listening for the sound of vehicles, hearing them and then seeing a dim light where the headlights should be as a darker shape materialized from the murk and faded into it.

Sometimes when I got home we would decide to have some fish and chips and I would set out for the shop. When I thought I must be getting near to it I would find the pavement edge and start to cross to the other side of the road or where I thought it was. In ordinary times, I would be across in a dozen strides but now it would seem an eternity until I could feel my feet touch the opposite pavement. I could tell from the feel of the pavement how near I was to the chip shop. Now there would be a dim light on my right, this was the shop's blackout curtain and I could smell the fish. Pushing through the blackout curtain I would enter the shop, which seemed unnaturally bright, then go back to the dark world outside.

One night coming from work I was approaching our passage or what I hoped would be our passage when a woman's voice spoke and I saw a darker figure in the gloom.

'Are you an ARP man?' the voice said and I recognized it as that of one of the two old Irish ladies.

I made myself known, and that I was not an Air Raid Precautions man, and I was implored to go into their flat because their cat had got a bone stuck in its throat. When I went in the other sister was holding the cat; with some trepidation I held its upper jaw open with one hand. The bone was a very large fishbone, but I was lucky and was able to draw it out without trouble, much to my relief and that of the cat. The sisters had great faith in me from then onwards. On such slender foundations are reputations made.

The blackout must have caused hundreds of deaths and injuries to the population before government saw fit to modify it. This was the period of what was called the Phoney War and in fact the blackout and ration books seemed to be the only things out of the ordinary. The Poles seemed to be the only people who were fighting and suffering, they and later the Finns. As far as the flats were concerned the thing that had most clearly shown that war was approaching was the construction of air-raid shelters in the yard, made of brick and concrete and looking like one-storey houses without windows.

A trickle of young men were being called up. Three of the lads in the Progress Office went. Raymond was an Englishman, but they put him in a Scottish regiment and when he came to see us in the New Year of 1940 he gave us a graphic account of how the men of the regiment were having to sleep in the snow of the Scottish Highlands. Norman, who had ambitions to be an actor, finished up in Palestine, while Denis proved his unsuitability for the infantry by losing his rifle. An understanding War Department, realizing his skill with cameras, transferred him to REME and the Rock of Gibraltar.

Anyone who paused for thought must have wondered how the war could end in an Allied victory since there seemed to be so little effort. To most people the best thing seemed to be to enjoy each day while so many things remained the same.

Frank Randle, that ribald old-time comedian, was in pantomime in Sheffield. Concerts were being held at the City Hall and at the University, *The Mikado* was at the Lyceum in March and *When we are Married* was playing there at the beginning of April, while on Easter Monday, 25 March, all the cinemas, and there were a lot of them at that time, were full. The easing of the blackout and the apparent freedom from air raids promoted this strange interlude, not only in Sheffield but all over the country.

The German invasion of Norway in April showed that the real war was starting, yet as late as 10 May my mother and I went on a coach trip to York. What was even stranger, this coach had a radio which kept up a flow of news bulletins and music. The news was of the German invasion of Belgium and Holland and I remember one of the last bulletins we heard was to the effect that Allied aircraft had made a massive intervention in the fighting which had stemmed the enemy advance. At least it can be said that in those desperate times we had people who knew how to write communiqués. I don't know if it was because of this trip, but at about this time I bought a tie for half-a-crown (12.5p in our present coinage).

There were events in my mother's family. The previous autumn her half-sister Nell was in a lorry taking women for the potato picking when it hit a bridge. Nell was thrown out and killed instantly.

About four years before the war, my mother's brother Jim lost his wife. By this time he was stone deaf and if only for this reason he needed a woman companion and missed the comforts of home very much. Soon a lively widow moved into his house. They had 'an understanding', as it would be put today, because remarriage would have penalized her financially. The following three or four years were the happiest of his life. Then in 1939 they went with a tour party to Scotland and among other passengers picked up en route was a blind man. He was an amusing companion and my uncle was persuaded to invite him to stay with them in Leicester. Jim's happiness was destroyed by his guest, who had no scruples about seducing the widow. If my uncle had been able to give vent to his anger by hitting the cuckoo in his nest I think the relationship would have survived, but how can you hit a blind man?

All this happened just before the war began. Uncle Jim came to stay with us at Christmas exactly a year after he had come with his mistress to spend the same season. In 1938 all had been gaiety, warmth, light, noise, music and people enjoying themselves in every pub, but in 1939 all was dark and silent and his mood too was gloomy and depressed.

Not long after the New Year opened we were delighted to hear that Jim had met someone he was going to marry. She was a doctor's housekeeper and they were to be married as soon as he had come out of hospital after a minor operation. He died unexpectedly and suddenly as he was getting out of bed in hospital. He had made a will only a few weeks before in which, having no children, he had divided his property between his prospective bride and the three surviving children of William Green, of whom my mother got the largest amount as Jim said he thought she was the poorest and most needy. Various items of crockery were included in the bequest as well as the money which, although really a small amount seemed to my mother a fortune, because she had never had anything.

My mother's half sister Susannah was also dead, but the rest of Susannah's family were still living at a house within sight of the farm.

At work, the new Shell Shop was in operation with female labour, and a night shift had been started in the Stamp Shop. Work was done in the bleakest conditions, for every door and skylight, every crack through which light and air could escape, was blocked. Conditions were indeed hellish.

Fumes and heat could not escape. By now everything was organized. All dies were now purchased, from one firm in Wednesbury, and the dark, thick, sticky stamping oil was now obtained from Kenneth Thelwall.

A lot of new people were moving into the factory from other occupations. A butcher came to work one of the Heller saws, a sporting journalist came as a Progress Chaser, together with a hire purchase man, the leader of a dance band and an inspector from Sun Alliance Insurance. We also had two Irishmen from Southern Ireland who came to work as labourers; they were contrasting types. One, whose name was Ryan, was a tall, handsome, dark young man, very talkative and apparently very attractive to women. His companion was a middle-aged stocky man who seldom spoke and who seemed to wear a permanent scowl on his face. They didn't seem to get on all that well together and it was reported that they had been seen fighting.

In the middle of 1940 the invasion threat and the increasing submarine menace caused the newspapers to comment on how useful it would be if the navy had the use of the Southern Irish ports and there was speculation that they might have to be seized by force if the situation got worse. As the lads ate their 'snap' and read their newspapers someone read out this suggestion, which met with general approval. Ryan stood up, his eyes flashing and said: 'I've got a rifle! I'll shoot the first Englishman dead who lands in Ireland!' It was not long after this episode that he and the sullen man returned to Ireland, presumably to prepare for an invasion.

At about this time quite a crowd of people used to get off the train at Millhouses Station, people who had boarded the train at Dronfield, and I usually found myself walking with them to the factory, where a number of the men worked in the Forge. I was amused on one of these mornings by a young girl with striking good looks who kept saying loudly and happily, 'There's nowt like a lad!'

To cope with all these new people everybody was issued with a little blue pass, a mini-passport with a photograph. In retrospect 1940 seemed a year of almost constant sunshine. I remember the lads from the Forge coming one very hot day out of the factory gates and picnicking on a grassy bank opposite. There was a report about bombs being dropped near the Houses of Parliament and some people said that they had heard explosions when the BBC news reader was reading the news. One of the hammer drivers said: 'BBC's near Parliament, tha' knows!' But I remember a morning when everyone was called to a meeting in the fitting shop. I think it was after France surrendered, when things were looking desperate and the weather was cool, overcast and grey, in tune with a desperate situation. The managing director, the works manager and other top brass were there. The managing director was a good speaker and I suppose he made some sort of pep speech, but all I remember now is that he finished with Herbert Morrison's phrase; 'Go to it!'

Work, we were told, was to carry on during air raid alerts and only cease during actual bombing. A man on the roof was to act as spotter to give warning when enemy aircraft approached. This lookout was a man I was to know quite well in the future but at the time I was struck by his serious, not to say funereal, appearance.

That September Susannah's family invited us over for a week. One night while we were there, the radio was switched on for the news. The announcer read out a report of the first night air raid on London; behind the deliberately discreet and sober words one sensed the horror of what had happened. For some reason we all went outside on the lawn. There was no light to be seen on the ground but the sky was ablaze with the light of many stars. It was silent, also. We returned to Sheffield full of foreboding.

During September, October and November life proceeded in the pattern to which we had become accustomed. There were air-raid warnings – four I think, in September, three in October, six in November, and after periods varying from half an hour to several hours, the all clear would sound without any sign of the enemy. The result was that people began to feel rather blasé, even though most of them reacted to the warning sirens as to a blow in the stomach.

At 7pm on 12 December, the sirens sounded as I was having a book stamped out in the Central Library. As I walked through the gloom home I was surprised by the zeal of the air-raid wardens and police calling out 'Take shelter.' I soon reached home and after a few minutes it was evident that this was going to be a very different night to those that followed the air-raid warnings we had had before.

There was the sound of aircraft overhead, the whistle of bombs, explosions and gunfire and, most ominous of all, a cascading noise of thousands of bricks as buildings collapsed. The women in the top flat came down to join us. On other occasions they had braved the sirens and waited for the all clear to come, but not this time. There was a knock at the passage door and a young woman rushed in. She worked at a firm near us and had been on her way home to Pitsmoor, but she dared go no farther and she knew my mother from working at the same firm. The violence and intensity of the raid seemed to increase minute by minute, the explosions seemed to be nearer to us, from time to time the whole building shook and the concrete floor trembled beneath our feet.

There still seemed something of normalcy while the electric light still burned and a small fire glowed in the grate. Then there was an explosion, the building shook, the light went out, there was a noise like a giant 'shoosh', and the glowing embers from the fire shot into the room accompanied by a great, blinding, choking, sulphurous cloud of soot.

As we gasped for breath we could see the night sky where the window had been. Someone said: 'Let's get into the shelter', but there was an obstruction in the passage doorway, the door itself had been blown off its hinges and was partially blocking the way. Eventually we struggled through and got into the yard.

It was quite light outside and not just from the sky – there was also the orange light of fires from the streets around us and the smell of burning. Inside the shelter the electric light lit the bare, cold space and the people from the other flats. There were stories of deaf people who wouldn't respond to warning shouts or answer the door however much the neighbours beat on it. It must have been between 10 and 11 pm that we had gone to the shelter. Soon afterwards, a party of young people arrived who had been at a dance. One girl seemed familiar and we realized that it

Lower High Street after bombing in December 1940

was the teenage girl from the Catholic family in the next passage, who was a natural blonde, but now dirt and soot had made her a brunette.

Bombs still rained down for hours and it was not until 4.20 a.m. that the all clear sounded and we could return home to find our flat uninhabitable. The night was cold and chill, although there were many fires. The church of St James was burning furiously and all the line of shops that had been in its shadow right to Vicar Lane had been burned down. We had seen the owner of the chip shop in the shelter weeping – not for her shop but for her cats.

Someone came round with word that buses were coming to take us away, and after what seemed a long time several arrived and drove a circuitous and roundabout way to a chapel in a district I had never seen before. It was a long journey avoiding unexploded bombs and streets made impassable by wreckage. We were taken into a schoolroom where arrangements were primitive, as there was no gas or electricity and there was only one small bowl of cold water to wash in. The place was nominally under the control of an elderly man, but he was in a state of shock and appeared stunned, and all the work was being done by some women.

Memory is very selective and the next thing I remember is setting off with my mother and walking home, she in a pair of carpet slippers. Walking down Cemetery Road we came to the end of that great shopping street, the Moor, and from there onwards was much destruction. Here we passed burnt-out trams, ruined shops, buildings still smoking. Among them I was sorry to notice the Central Cinema, where I had seen *The Private Life of Henry VIII* when it first came out.

Finally we got to the flats but there were police, guarding against looters, who were turning people away. They gave us ten minutes or so to collect what we needed out of the wreckage. Then I went to the Town Hall where I was told that people from the flats were being moved to a reception centre. I realize now as I did not then, how hard all these officials, police, wardens, etc., worked at this time, themselves tired and short of sleep. Our destination turned out to be the large modern school at High Storrs. Here we were given blankets and a place on a classroom floor, but everyone was so tired we would have slept anywhere. In our room there was a very interesting man who had served at the end of the Great War and just after in a very unusual theatre of war – Persia, or Iran as it is now called. He spoke in a very staccato way, relying on his ability to make excellent sketches to explain what he meant. There was a blackboard with some chalk in our room and he used to make drawings as he talked. 'Kurds dress like this, this is their headdress! Bakhtiari like this. This is what the Persians at this place looked like!'

After a night's sleep I decided to walk from Ecclesall to where I worked at Millhouses to see if the factory was still intact. The way was all downhill and it didn't take me long to get there. I soon saw that quite a lot of damage had occurred at Millhouses – the house and shop where I got my morning paper had vanished, another shop nearby had been hit and the two sisters who ran it had been killed.

I walked along past Millhouses station and to my place of employment, which I was glad to see was intact. When I walked down the drive I noticed a great silence, just a few human voices, for there was no gas or electricity. My boss, Maurice, was delighted to see me and provided me with something I really longed for – a bucket of hot water with which to wash the grime and soot from my face. The hot water had been heated on the blacksmiths' hearth. Some of the smiths were doing real work but one hearth was permanently occupied with boiling water for the canteen on the coke fire. Women from the canteen kept coming with giant kettles and mashing tea in them. Maurice got a shovel from somewhere, cleaned it and

Salvaging furniture after the Blitz in December 1940

then cooked some bacon on it. I have eaten bacon since that tasted as good, but none better.

Bill, the ex-footballer, who was in charge of the night shift, had been on his way to work from his house in Darnall when the raid started. He took refuge in a shelter under a building which was set on fire, and molten lead from the roof splashed all down the back of his coat as he made his escape. For years afterwards he wore that coat splashed with lead.

We had three air-raid alarms while we were at High Storrs, one of which was a considerable attack on the East End, and as we sat in the school shelters the sound of bombs was partially drowned by the firing of the anti-aircraft guns near the school.

We were delighted to be able to return to our flat at Christmas. The water supply had been restored on Christmas Eve, the passage door had been put back and the window had been restored in a fashion, that is the window space was covered by a large piece of wood in which was a tiny square of what people called 'crazy' glass, which was transparent but only just. Here we ate our Christmas dinner of stewed steak, slept on the floor and thanked God.

CHAPTER SIXTEEN

# WAR YEARS

The two great air raids of December 1940 were never to be repeated. At the time, though, we did not know this and in 1941 alone there were at least forty-four air-raid warnings and in some cases bombs were dropped. All but about half a dozen of these alerts happened before the German invasion of Russia took place. I remember there was a warning at about a quarter past midnight on 12 August, which lasted for some two hours, and I remember one man expressing the common feeling by saying about Hitler: 'I reckon he's shit his potfull.'

But in the New Year everyone expected a new onslaught and all sorts of preparations went on. In January we got tin hats and on 25 February, the day before my birthday, I got an unexpected present, a stirrup pump, which I had to store in our flat. Earlier than this on 7 February the men of the flats who formed the Firewatching Unit had held a meeting at which the following points were agreed upon.
1. Practise with ladders until accustomed to them.
2. Use rope for hauling ladders to the top landing although hauling up involves the danger of dropping them.
3. Cut notches in ladder for points of placing.
4. Which first? The pump or the ladder.
5. Learn one another's addresses.
6. Find out heights of landings.
7. Remember passages.
8. Get to know about the roofs.

I must say I am glad that we never had to perform any of the tasks envisaged in the programme, for the height of the flats from ground level to roof level must have been well over 60 feet. Before the war, for a wager, a young man had walked on top of the roof on the Hawley Street side from one end to the other. I never had any desire to follow his example.

Two people came to give us some simple training, such as crawling on hands and knees through smoke-filled rooms, in this case the air-raid shelters. The trainers consisted of a very comely young woman with blonde hair and a very enthusiastic young man. At the end of our last lesson, we men of the flats stood in a group watching the receding figures of our trainers when a romantic spirit piped up: 'Do you think he's sweet on her?'

There was a moment's embarrassed silence, then one of the older men said: 'Anyway, it's nowt to do with us.'

It is surprising how quickly calamities can be repaired. By 4 January the trams were running again to Millhouses; I can't remember now how I got there in the interval. The ruined shops got patched up, or else moved into other premises. Walshs, the mighty and glamorous store of my youth where there had been music, was just a huge blackened tangle of wreckage, but one department moved to Church Street, and others to Broomhill.

Some people were not successful in continuing their business. Mac, who had operated a newsagents and tobacconists at the bottom of Vicar Lane, strove to carry on for a while, spreading his wares on the spot where his shop had been, but not for long.

While people were coping with physical damage, shock to the nervous system inflicted more lasting wounds. The two Welsh sisters who had worked for the church suffered a frightening experience in their little house in Sheaf Garden Terrace. They had to be dug out of the cellar of the house, when bombs aimed at the railway yard struck their street. I went to see them in the one room they occupied at 35 Broomhall Place. Janey, the younger sister, had recovered her poise but the old lady was no longer in the world mentally. She lay in bed, quite motionless, not uttering a sound, her eyes staring unseeingly at the window. Poor little woman, all who knew her were glad when she slipped gently into lasting sleep.

The burning of St James's was a bitter blow for the Vicar, Mr Parsons. For nearly thirty years his ministry had kept the church open and preserved one of Sheffield's most interesting buildings. He did not long survive his church's ruin.

At the Golden Ball, the pub building had survived intact but the licensee was suffering from shock and within a year or so he had handed over to a new man.

From the time we got a wireless set after the death of George V, I had become a music lover. The war years were in many ways a golden age of music in Sheffield when there was every sort available at reasonable prices. I used to go to the weekly classical concerts at the City Hall as well as concerts by military bands there and in the parks. I went to the Victoria Hall to the chamber music concerts sponsored by John Parr, an elderly gentleman who had been a bassoon player in the Hallé Orchestra. There

Sheffield High Street in flames during the Blitz of December 1940

were many interesting novelties in his programmes, one of them I remember being a piece by Mozart for two bassoons, called *Moorish Tower Music*. 'Chamber music' was a dirty word in those days and I remember old Mr Parr standing up to introduce the programme to about six or seven people and saying: 'As you see I do not expect to make my fortune with these concerts but everybody has a hobby, some bet on horses, some watch football, mine is music.'

Now that I was in work and slightly more prosperous I decided to get some false teeth. I was happy to part with twenty-five of my own teeth, which had caused me nothing but pain all my life. In August 1941 I was measured for a new suit, which cost me £5 2s 6d and in October I acquired a new hat for 8s 6d.

On the 28 September 1941, when I was setting out for work, I captured a goat that was wandering on the tram track at the beginning of Church Street. I took it to the police box at the side of the Town Hall in Surrey Street. I rang from the outside phone and got in touch with police headquarters and convinced them that I had not found a coat. After about ten minutes a tired looking policeman with a resigned expression came and took charge of my captive. Alas, I never learned where it had come from or what happened to it.

I made a new friend about this time. Ernest lived in one of the passages below us and was a penknife maker, a devout Christian and an officer in the Church Lads Brigade. It was this latter activity that first drew my attention to him, for he had a very loud penetrating voice with which he issued commands. When I commented on this, people who knew him would laugh and say: 'That's a landlord's voice.' Indeed his father had been the landlord of a pub and Ernest told me that it was helping his father in the early morning to open the doors and windows of the pub to let the stink of beer out that made him a teetotaller. In the Great War he had been a mechanic in the Royal Flying Corps in Mesopotamia and India, under his hero Colonel Tennant. He served in the days when the mechanic who had serviced a plane had to go up with the kite on its next flight. He loved music and went to as many concerts as he could, but he was performing fire-watching duties not only at the cutlery firm where he worked but also at the cathedral as a volunteer. No wonder that when he died his ashes were placed in the cathedral.

As the year wore on and there were no major air raids we began to count our good fortune in that only part of the Hawley Street end of our flats had been chipped away by a bomb and the occupants had not been seriously injured – they being a man who took fruit and vegetables round the district on a horse drawn dray, and his wife and daughter. We had been more fortunate than people in the other block, at least one of whom had been killed when a bomb ripped away part of the corner of the building at Silver Street Head.

The country was filling up with people from overseas. In July, coming back from Leicester, we got on a train full of young Canadian soldiers – friendly, good-natured lads, who seemed thrilled to be in the Old Country. I've often wondered how many lived to go back to Canada.

After the Blitz I stopped taking sandwiches to work and started having lunch at the Waggon and Horses Tea Rooms on the edge of Millhouses Park. There was a very pleasant walk there from the factory, down a flight of steps into the park and on past the cricket field. Mr Haig, who was the manager, and his wife performed miracles with limited resources in food but some of the wartime provender was very poor stuff, notably the nasty, sour-tasting sausage. A blind man, or Rip van Winkle waking from his long sleep, would have known what day it was from the menu; shepherds' pie or 'hunt the meat', as it was called, appeared on at least one day a week. As the time approached 1 pm, the buzz of conversation, the rattle of cutlery and even the sounds of teeth and jaws chomping and grinding food would cease as the radio time signal would be followed by Today's Cairo Communiqué about the fighting in North Africa. It was during the evening news bulletin about Wavell's victory that the heaviest bombing had started on the 12 December the year before. This time, not long after I had started going to the tea rooms, a rather innocent-sounding item occurred in the communiqué to the effect that our forces had made contact at El Ageila with some German troops under a General Rommel. Before I leave the Waggon and Horses for a while it is sobering to note that in July 1941 the price of lunch there was 1s 6d (7½p in present-day money), and this covered a main dish with vegetables and a very pleasant sweet, apple pie with custard, etc.

In 1941, for the first time, people began to think the war might have an end and that the end might be victory. In the factory a steady routine had developed, with more women arriving, some men being called up, and other men from diverse occupations being directed to work in the firm, which gave a bit of variety. All the men in the Forge were in a reserved occupation. Our lads enjoyed being regarded by the other workers in the firm as a rough, tough bunch, working in hot, dirty, dangerous conditions. Occasionally they would march off to the canteen, all sweat and dirt, and stride straight in ahead of everyone else as soon as the door was opened.

Of new arrivals, there was one man who drove from Eyam in Derbyshire every day, another man was a tailor who was also a champion draughts player, so much so that he claimed to have an opening named after him. We also had people coming back. The young man from the Buying Office came back from training for the submarine service; his boat was returning to port from a training exercise and was on the surface when an enemy fighter machine-gunned the deck and Percy was hit in the arm, resulting in his being invalided from the navy.

By this time a number of stores were in existence in the factory stocking everything from finished parts to steel, so it was no surprise when it was announced that a stores controller had been appointed. Everybody was thunderstruck when it was learned that the new controller was to be the former inspector from Sun Alliance Insurance who had proved to be an indifferent progress chaser. People were even more astonished when Arthur said that the works manager told him he had been chosen despite being unpopular because people who did their job right were always unpopular. Most of us thought this a very questionable idea. One has to admit that he discharged his task quite well, but any improvements in organization were more than balanced by delays and ill feeling caused by his intolerable arrogance, bluster and bombast. Away from the factory, though, he was said to be a brilliant weapons instructor in the Home Guard.

Somewhere about this time the Government gave its blessing to joint production committees of workers and managers. In our factory this committee had eight members who were known as 'The Big Eight'. I don't know what benefits rose from their labours but I know one thing, it certainly enlarged some people's egos.

I have never smoked myself, but watching the Machine Shop Superintendent before and during the war I came to realize what a useful instrument a pipe is for delaying tactics; whenever Tom had to deliver a judgement or someone came in with an unexpected problem his pipe would have gone out and several seconds or maybe a couple of minutes would elapse while Tom struck matches and took great puffs at his pipe until it was drawing satisfactorily and he could devote his time to the difficulty on hand.

During my early years at the factory I avoided as much as possible a fierce-looking man with a bristly white military moustache – I thought he looked like a sergeant major, and that in fact was what he had been. George was his name and he was in charge of Goods Inward, checking and booking in everything that entered. The truth was that for a long time he was terribly overworked and he hadn't time to spend on courtesy. During the war he seemed to mellow and would talk about his days in the army. Like many old soldiers he said little about his service in the Great War but he liked to talk about his years in the old regular army which in his case extended back to the South African War. Most of what he told me I have forgotten, but I remember him saying that out of your pay of a shilling a day you could save a farthing. He gave a comical account of the departure of his battalion for South Africa, from either Belfast or Dublin. He described the big crowd cheering them as they came out of the barrack gate, 'and all the Irish whores weeping their eyes out'. His regiment was a Yorkshire regiment. He seemed such a lively if peppery person that I was really shocked when he was found dead at home; and so I learned no more about the old army.

An even older man who died about this time was Harry, from one of the western counties. For most of his life he had worked in the gardens of some of the great houses but according to his own account his main interest in life was chasing women – the servant girls who kept the big houses alive. He called himself the 'Norton Poet' and used to produce newspaper cuttings of verses he said he had won prizes for, which were somewhat different from those he composed to recite for the entertainment of the stampers at lunch time. He was very active for a man of about 80 but he was knocked down in Woodseats during the blackout and although he recovered he was never the same man again and within a few months he was dead.

At the end of 1940 we got a lad from London in the Stamp Shop. I think he had had some bad experiences in the London Blitz; it had left him practically dumb. He hardly ever spoke, although he understood what was said to him. Nowadays people would call him a 'zombie' but we all called him 'Bomber'. Most of the men and lads treated him with sympathy and forbearance but halfway through the war a drop stamper arrived who was a nasty man, a bully whom everyone was afraid of. Bomber was assigned as hammer driver to this new man. The new man was a very good worker, producing first-class stampings, but he had a foul mouth which he used on poor Bomber and a sadistic streak. The drivers, apart from their official share of the piecework, were also given some money by their particular stampers – 'Natty Money' it was called, which varied according to the generosity of their mates. Bomber's mate used to throw the silver coins forming the Natty Money into the tin of thick, black, sticky, smelly stamping oil at the side of the hammer and leave Bomber to get it out somehow. After the war, when this particular stamper left, there was a great sense of relief. There was a young lad who came as a trimmer who talked to himself all the time. I don't think the bombing could be blamed for his state of mind. Someone asked him who he was talking to and he said it was a little old man who was telling him that he must kill somebody. After a time he was taken away and we all felt safer.

About this time we had a lad called Vic, who was a lazy, unreliable character who eventually ceased coming to work. Then a few days later he turned up in uniform, alleging he had joined an infantry regiment and expressing the hope that his workmates would make a collection for him as they usually did for former workmates who had joined the services.

'Where's your paybook?' said Yanks.

'They haven't given me one yet,' Vic said.

'I don't believe you,' said Yanks and he was right.

A few days later the truth came out in a report in the local paper. Our hopeful warrior had been brought to court for buying a uniform from a deserter and obtaining money by false pretences.

During the war we often worked a seven-day week, and one Sunday in October 1942 we got word that we had to go to the canteen for a special announcement. It was of course to tell us of the North African landings and we came away feeling that at last things were on the move and we were striking at the enemy. Up to then it had just been the bombers that had been our only means of striking at the Germans. We felt it was only right that German cities should suffer as ours had done, although there was the knowledge that the bomber attacks involved the loss of many young men.

Setting off for a day in the parks, summer 1942

There was a girl on the firm, a clerk, whose boyfriend, a pilot, together with the crew of his Hampden bomber, never returned from a mission. For months and months she kept making inquiries, hoping against hope that he was a prisoner or perhaps had survived and escaped overland. But it was not to be. From that day to this nothing has come to light as to his fate.

During 1943 the country started filling up with Americans and still more came in 1944 as a cross-Channel invasion of occupied France drew near.

During 1944 our firm, like other plants up and down the country, became involved in a patriotic exercise called 'Daughter of the Regiment', a sort of beauty contest to select a girl who would grace various rallies and events intended to raise the spirits of the people. From the numerous young girls who worked at a variety of occupations, the judges chose a lovely, charming and intelligent maiden who was well fitted to be the 'Daughter of the Regiment', but in the event she married an American soldier, so perhaps the US army benefited.

In this year 1944 our personnel officer, who was a Francophile, steeped in French language and culture, brought a friend of hers to teach the rudiments of the language to a small class who met on the top floor of the office block. This lady was a Czech married to an American and she said, apropos of the English and the Americans: 'It's a pity you have the same language for you have nothing else in common.' Too true, I'm afraid. The English have the sense, the Americans the power and the dough.

Change was in the air and not everyone looked forward to it. One such was a slim, dapper, good-looking man who hailed from Jamaica. He was a white man and for the greater part of the war he worked in the Inspection Department and lunched at the Waggon and Horses. He seemed the odd man out in his department, very immaculate and smartly dressed, very correct in his language but not a mixer. I spoke to him about conditions in Jamaica. No, he wasn't afraid of hurricanes! They got plenty of warning! Earthquakes terrified him! When the earth was moving up and down like someone shaking a rug! At the end of the war he came to shake hands. He was going back to Jamaica. 'I expect when I get back there will be a black police superintendent. In my day they were never allowed to rise above sergeant.'

CHAPTER SEVENTEEN

# PEOPLE AND PLACES

Now I shall describe events in my own life and changes in the flats and in the districts around us, in the period from the end of 1941 to the end of 1945.

Not long after the North African landings in October 1942 I went to Bramall Lane Football Ground for a 'medical'. I was classed grade 3, which I found vaguely humiliating, but on the other hand I was pleased to find the colour of my eyes described as 'green'. My official height of five feet and half an inch came as no surprise. I was surprised by the interest aroused by my shins; because of the effects of the rickets I had suffered from as a child they had an appearance called 'sabre edge' and it seemed to fascinate the doctors, who called me back to stand in a sort of wooden sentry box while they stood at a distance and tried to imprint my appearance on their minds. I heard someone say: 'Rickety, Dr Roper, or would you call it rackety?'

Thus I never served in any of His Majesty's Forces but I did go to various places to do firewatching, all of them rather seedy workshops belonging to 'Little Mesters'. One belonged to a man who put the serrations in saws, a very skilled trade. There was another man who did firewatching at the same place – a thin, middle-aged, poorly looking man, who said that he never slept. He had a complaint, he said, which prevented him from sleeping and all he could do was to sit in a chair, well wrapped up, and talk and talk. He was a very well-read man and a good conversationalist but with having to set off for Millhouses for my day's work an hour or so after finishing the watch, I didn't look forward to doing my turn with him, after the first few nights. The owner of the business and I were both sceptical about him never sleeping but it had to be conceded that he never to our knowledge closed his eyes.

After a time I was transferred to a place somewhere near Carver Street. I don't think I ever saw this particular 'Little Mester' because there was a sort of permanent watchman there, an elderly retired miner whose stories of hardship, injury and fights in the mines I listened to with interest. One of his favourite remarks was: 'If tha works in't pit tha's got to be able to go a bit.'

There was another man who used to come whom I remember very well. He was a little man, nearly bald, who had only one tooth in his head. 'If I lose that I'm finished,' he said, and explained that he was a Punch and Judy man who anchored the gadget that he used to produce Mr Punch's funny voice to his remaining tooth and it was essential to the business. He came of a gypsy family, he said; he and his wife, carrying their props on their backs, used to walk to the seaside, sleeping in barns and fields and giving Punch and Judy shows on the way to raise money to buy food to live on. He had a printing business now which was his main source of income. When trade was bad he begged cardboard boxes from the shops and got the girls who worked for him chopping the cardboard up into squares on which they printed his name and address and the kind of work he was willing to perform. He then sent the girls out delivering the printed squares all over Sheffield. He did not praise the girls who worked for him, 'snotty-nosed buggers', but they were always the best workers in his experience. Now he no longer needed to work. His family wanted him to retire but if he did that would be the end. It was work that kept him going.

In the vicinity of the flats there was a change at the Golden Ball when 'Sam' took over as landlord. By now the American soldiers had become an important source of income to everybody in the leisure industry. Sam had a sign put up just inside the door on the Townhead Street front of the building that said: 'This is Sams.' I remember coming past the door one day when a crowd of Yanks were being guided by one of their number who had discovered the Golden Ball, and as they entered a short, fat man like a Midwest farmer in uniform exclaimed in a throaty voice: 'So this is Sams!' Throughout the remainder of the war and just afterwards it was a gathering place for the GIs and their counterparts in the US Air Force.

Coming home in the evenings I would get off the tram at the Town Hall and walk along Leopold Street, and every doorway would be occupied by a girl hoping to pair off with a Yank and squeeze some of the money with which they all seemed to be well supplied from him. I couldn't help thinking what a poor opinion the Yanks must have of us when every hand was stretched out to relieve them of their dough, including shopkeepers, bartenders and others who played on their unfamiliarity with our coinage to fleece them. One used to hear of men coming out of shops and their girlfriends checking their change and sending them back for the remainder. Coming home once in a crowded train I stood in the corridor watching with amusement the tactics of an elderly man who was obviously trying to scrounge anything he could get from an American who was smoking by the open window. After trying various ploys without success, like praising American cigarettes, how much better they were than ours, the old chap to keep the conversation alive said something like: 'I see you like fresh air. So do I.' The Yank, puffing away, said indifferently: 'Sure! There's nothin like it!'

The war itself had now become something one read about in the papers or listened to on the radio but I think it was just about Christmas 1944 that there had been an air-raid warning, caused it was said by a discharge of 'Doodle Bugs' and there was another air-raid alert on the 4 March 1945, but nothing happened.

During these years there was very little that wasn't rationed – food, clothes, sweets, etc. The shopkeeper with whom you traded, in our case the people who had the half moon-shaped shop at the bottom of Townhead Street, needed to have a pair of sharp scissors to cut out all the various coupons from the ration book. Then they had all the problems associated with very small quantities of some delicacy like tinned fruit or salmon arriving and how did you share twelve tins among one hundred and fifty customers? Things would be kept under the counter until the shop was empty and it was safe to give the item to the favoured customer, but the favoured customer then had to go without next time.

It was now that we learned of horrors like tinned carrots and macon – mutton made into an imitation bacon – that didn't last long. Some new foods were quite nice, like snoek – which someone told me was a South African name for barracuda – and spam, a tinned meat said to cause children to talk of Uncle Spam. With greengrocers, it was not the shopkeepers' unofficial rationing of delicacies but the other system, you can have tomatoes if you buy carrots, you can have apples if you buy turnips. At the end of the war an old favourite turned up in a peculiar guise, dried bananas, a hard black substance supposed to be good for you.

In addition to music, the other arts flourished. The Playhouse had reopened but the only plays I can recall seeing there at this time were Shaw's *Getting Married* and *Britannia of Billingsgate*. Everything (but the titles) has faded from my mind. I saw *Hamlet* at Arnold Freeman's Little Theatre near the Royal Infirmary. It was a tense and exciting performance by an amateur cast. There was also Donald Wolfit and his company at the Lyceum in *Richard III* and at the International Settlement which I had just joined, I saw *Lady Precious Stream*, a play in Chinese style with concessions to Western taste.

The International Settlement on Wellesley Road was an interesting place to go to in those days, its membership included German Jews, Czechs, Poles, and other nationalities, and the programme included classics of the silent film like *The Cabinet of Dr Caligari* and gramophone recitals of operas one was never likely to see, like *Cosi fan tutte*.

We had plenty of music in the city and I am glad to think we still have, unlike the theatre. On 5 October 1944 we had Beecham and the London Philharmonic Orchestra and there was Malcolm Sargent and other conductors, and most notably Barbirolli, who had left a lucrative job in New York to conduct the Hallé. I still remember the occasion when he conducted Verdi's *Manzoni Requiem*, which was given added poignancy by the death of Franklin Delano Roosevelt a few days before.

During 1944 and 1945 the sports club of the firm I worked for and the International Settlement both had enthusiastic chess players and feeling I ought to be in the swim I too acquired a board, chessmen and books on chess, but I soon discovered I would never be much of a player. It seemed to me that to be any good you had to devote your whole life to it, and that I was not prepared to do. Jim, the tailor, who had been directed to our firm, developed into a good chess player and attracted the attention of the company secretary, who was a lifelong devotee of the game. The secretary succeeded in getting Jim transferred to Costing. I was pleased for his sake but I was rather annoyed by the report that came back to me on the grapevine that the secretary had said: 'We must replace Jim! We must find William a horsefaced woman.'

In August 1944 we went to Boston for a week's holiday. Apart from visiting our relatives at Leicester this was the first time we had been away anywhere since the war began. Billy the blacksmith had given us the address of the widow with whom we stopped; it was a small terrace house by the river bank, quite pleasant and central. All day Saturday and all day Sunday the rain poured down relentlessly; it was impossible to go out so on Sunday our hostess decided to provide us with some entertainment in the shape of hymn tunes played on the piano by her daughter, who was a teacher.

When the rain did cease and we were able to explore Boston we found it a very interesting place, quite apart from St Botolph's, the magnificent 'Stump'. We went in the beautiful eighteenth century Fydell House, only part of which could be seen, as the Women's Voluntary Service (WVS) occupied some of it. The roof was covered by sheets and apparently had been on fire. We had a look in the museum on a chill, dank day and its state was as depressing as the weather. Everything was covered by a layer of dust and the identification labels were yellow with age. By day and night there was the sound of aircraft engines and as long as there was light one could see formations of aircraft streaming outwards to the continent and others flying home to base.

This was the period of the 'Bevin Boy' scheme when youngsters had the choice of working in the pits as an alternative to joining the services. The future husband of one of my cousins had taken this option and we were informed he was at a training establishment at Woodhouse, a village I had never heard of before. We were able to make his stay at Woodhouse entertaining; he was a keen footballer and so I came to see the only two games of professional football I have ever attended at Bramall Lane. (When I was at school in the 1920s I used to go to watch the Sheffield School Sports at 'The Lane'.) Because of the war, football had been regionalized and Sheffield United were playing in what was called the Northern Section. United were playing Barnsley and not having our Bevin Boy's keen sight I couldn't make out what was happening. We seemed to be a long way from the action. There didn't seem to be very many people where we were. Near us was a middle-aged man who stood silently for a long time and then suddenly opened his mouth and said in a quiet voice, without much conviction: 'Up Barnsley'. Then he remained silent for a long time and repeated the performance. For me, the worst moment – one that fixed my aversion to football matches – was getting out of the ground. There was such a scrum at the entrance I thought I was going to be crushed to death.

Among my visits to musical, theatrical and variety performances I went to a very interesting event in the Graves Art Gallery on the 3 March 1945, when John Piper gave a talk entitled *Topographical Illustration*. Piper was then a tall thin man with a long, narrow face and a large thin nose. The gallery in which the lecture took place was lined with pictures of Renishaw Hall and its grounds, painted by Piper for Sir Osbert Sitwell, who introduced the talk. Sir Osbert said that in England we tended to regard pictures as ordeals to be endured or moral examples rather than things to be enjoyed. John Piper made a rather pleasant gesture at the end of the programme when he thanked the attendant in charge of the projector; he said it was the first time nothing had gone wrong with it during one of his lectures.

Victory in Europe Day (VE Day), 8 May, was rather strange, for although a lot of bunting and flags had been put out there seemed to be a lack of cheerfulness. People seemed apathetic, tired and indifferent, and even the sky was dull and in the afternoon it poured with rain. In the evening, however, after the pubs opened, people's spirits rose and great crowds assembled round the Town Hall to listen to the Salvation Army Band.

At the Golden Ball there was a great crowd of people, a lot of noise and many fights. Girls from the Land Army were testing their soberness by walking on the kerb stones. Sam the landlord gave up trying to keep order in the pub and walked across the road to where we were standing at the end of the passage and kept saying pathetically: 'How would you like my job? I don't know how I am going to get them out at eleven.' By this time he was in the self-pitying stage of drunkenness and kept stroking his bald head, but somehow or other he did manage to empty the pub.

On 17 May my neighbour Ernest and I took the stirrup pumps issued to the flats to St Mark's Crescent, the collection centre. We really felt that the nightmare of war had been lifted from us, at least in Europe.

After reports of the atomic bombs on Japan and rumours of peace I was getting shaved when it was announced on the 7 am news that VJ Day had been declared as from midnight on 14 August, and in the evening I walked among the crowds in Barker's Pool, where fireworks were being let off. Now we had to see what peace would be like.

# CHAPTER EIGHTEEN

# CALAMITY AND CHANGE

My mother had for years been suffering with the ulcers on her legs. By September 1945 these were septic on both legs and her life was in danger. Our Scottish doctor had gone to Australia, his successor had been called up, and we now went to a doctor who had a surgery on Gell Street. He was a man of few words who used to listen to his patients, grunting occasionally and interjecting the infrequent word or phrase. He brought in a specialist who got my mother into the Royal Hospital, a jumble of buildings now demolished. Here the ulcers were treated with penicillin, the new wonder drug. I was told that they needed to use so much that the hospital ran out of stock. I had been to the Royal from time to time to see people I knew who had spent time there. It must have been a porter's nightmare, with changes in floor level and ramps to be negotiated. When mother came out of hospital in October, one leg was in plaster and she had to use crutches until April 1946.

In March 1946, petrol was 2s a gallon and black market petrol 5s. I toyed with the idea of buying a car, but as it would cost at least £60 to buy a second-hand one, there was nowhere to garage it, I was no mechanic and there would be other expenses involved, I did not pursue the idea.

The thought had been put in my mind by a fellow office worker who was known as 'The Snake' and who had like all of us received a small rise in wages which caused him to say: 'I think steady young fellows like us might be able to run a car.' I had never thought of myself as a 'steady young fellow'.

We visited my mother's country – the Deepings in Lincolnshire – in September 1946, being transported there and back by private hire car.

Mother *c.* 1947 at the age of 65 years

When we came back we adopted a black-and-white cat which up to then we had called White Paws but which because of its relish for potatoes we now called Spud.

The penicillin which had saved mother's life and legs had unpleasant side-effects. From time to time and without warning she would become violently sick and completely helpless, and it would take a couple of days for her to recover. Several years passed by before the effects of the drug wore off.

As if to compensate for the continuing shortages and rationing there were many artistic events, music, films and so on in Sheffield in the first few years after the war ended. Apart from the Philharmonic concerts, which celebrated their tenth anniversary on the 24 August 1945, there was the Carl Rosa company in opera at the Empire in July 1946 and a year later at the same theatre I saw *La Bohème* and *Carmen*. Despite war damage there were still a lot of cinemas showing some really outstanding films, although the Electra in Fitzallan Square closed as a conventional cinema at the end of July 1945 and re-opened in September as a News Theatre. The Graves Art Gallery was home to many interesting exhibitions during those years.

We certainly needed something to brighten our lives. In March 1946 we had no coal and we burned every wooden thing we could spare and pieces of cardboard as well. Our neighbours were very good and helped us as much as they could, although they too were short of fuel. The next year, 1947, the cold was worse and fuel even scarcer. We could only keep warm by burning chairs and going to bed early.

Small things showed that changes were taking place. In May 1946 I found the newsagent was able to let me have the *Daily Telegraph* again after more than four years when it was unobtainable. During the first two years of peace many things changed in our flats and at work, but one thing did not alter. The air-raid shelters remained in the yard, gradually getting filthier and harbouring vermin. People were afraid to leave their doors open in case they were invaded by mice or worse. Folk used to say of the shelters: 'They're keeping 'em for next time!'

At work, the end of the war brought technical developments in production and changes among the workforce. One change was invisible to us but it affected not only the Forge but the whole factory. Ours was an old-established firm whose roots lay in the Victorian railway industry. It had gradually declined after the Great War until it was taken over by T.W. Ward, a collector of failing companies. T.W. Ward, 'Tommy Ward' as Sheffielders called it, was part of the folklore of the city, the tale of the man who rose from pushing a wheelbarrow collecting scrap to affluence.

Our factory was now linked to the car industry and was part of a group of companies most of which were in the West Midlands. We lower members of the staff were invited to a splendid dinner at a hotel, celebrating the formation of the new group. On arrival we were greeted with a handshake and a glass of wine by the overlord of the new group. After the dinner had been consumed there was a series of speeches by the chairman, sundry directors and members of the upper crust. Apart from those from the chairman and the managing director the level of speeches seemed very low. There was a great deal of nostalgia expressed and the phrase 'I well remember' featured at least twice in every speech. To do him justice, the new chairman seemed a man of enlightened views. He introduced a shares scheme for the employees and a club for those who had served the firm for twenty-five years, after which they would be given a gold watch.

With the ending of the war there was an exodus of those who had been

Laycocks' presentation to Tommy Plant, *c.* 1955. George is on the extreme left

directed into industry by the Ministry of Labour and at the same time others who had been tied to their jobs left to seek greener pastures and higher wages or in some cases to set up their own businesses. Bill, the ex-footballer, who had been in charge of the night shift in the Forge and Drop Stamp department throughout the war was so sick of the heat, dirt and fumes that he was determined to take up any job that would give him the chance of escape. In the event he bought a boarding house at Blackpool. Three of the die sinkers left, two to start up on their own and the third to go to Australia where he said he intended to shoot crocodiles.

As the old hands went, new recruits came from other parts of the world. At one time we had three Somalis working in the shop. They were tall, slim, handsome men, with glistening, pale coffee-coloured bodies. Two of them were cousins; one of the cousins, the older one, was very tall, a magnificent looking and highly intelligent young man and remarkably self-assured. He said his father owned a fleet of taxis in Berbera, in British Somaliland. The younger of the two was neither as tall nor as mature as his cousin. He was like a large overgrown boy with a very equable temperament. This was just as well because some of the English teenagers liked to play tricks on him. Their favourite trick was to creep up behind him and touch his private parts, when this happened he used to leap about three feet in the air amid howls of laughter. After a time the Somalis left. I've often wondered if any of them still survive after independence, wars, famines and dictatorship.

A year or so after the war ended the Poles began to arrive. They seemed to be mostly men who had fought in Italy and introduced us to the odd Italian phrase. There were about half a dozen of them in our shop. They seemed to thrive on hard work. When they first came there seemed to be unlimited work for everybody but a time came when work fell off and the English began to resent the Poles working so much overtime. 'We don't want the Roly-polys getting all the overtime,' they told my boss.

Just after the Poles in our department had been set on, another Pole arrived whom Maurice decided to employ since he seemed to be a skilled, useful man. As soon as word of this leaked out the other Poles stopped work, marched to the office and said they wouldn't work with the new recruit. He was not a Pole, they said, but a German. This ended the affair.

On the whole the Poles fitted in quite well. Most trouble was caused by quarrels among themselves, and most of that by Stanislas or Stan, who was one of two Poles who worked as strikers for English blacksmiths. Tony, the other Polish striker, was a tall, quiet young man who usually ignored Stan as he shouted insults (presumably) in Polish, but one day Stan came to where Tony was working and chalked some Polish words on the anvil. They had an immediate effect. Snatching up his striking hammer Tony chased his tormentor round the shop. If he had caught him there would have been a violent death.

Stan seemed to be a man always looking for a fight and Tony was not the only fellow Pole with whom he crossed swords in the factory. Away from work he must also have been in conflict, because one week he failed to come to work for several days. This was something unheard of, for whatever else he was there was no doubt he was a good worker. When he turned up it was evident he had been in a fight and it transpired that the police had found him unconscious in the gutter in a street in a district like Pitsmoor to the north of the city.

One consequence of our firm becoming part of a group was that our works manager went most years to the USA, coming back primed with ideas for improving our performance. One of the first fruits of these transatlantic visits was the replacement of the blacksmiths' coke hearths by gas furnaces. 'People will think we're shoeing horses,' said the manager – so out went the hearths, in came the gas furnaces. The blacksmiths had to accept the fact although they knew that for their work, hardening tools and so on, coke was best, enabling a greater range of heat, a more delicate

Laycocks, *c.* 1950. Back row (on left), left to right: –?–, Hadfield, McCall, Burden, Young, Cartwright. Middle row: –?–, –?–, Johnson, –?–, Cooney, Smith. On wall: Ledger, O'Connor, Rowe, Dickinson, Revill. Front row: Broadhead, C. Bower, J. Bower

variation of temperature. I suppose the 'breeze' coke itself would have become more difficult to obtain as more firms went over to gas.

The rope slings by which the drop hammer heads were lifted and dropped were replaced by steel bands. This was an improvement in some ways but if the band came off or parted then it would fly curling and writhing like an angry snake, its edges as sharp as razor blades, capable of cutting off a man's head if he was in the way. Maurice, my boss, was hit by one – he had a nasty cut on one arm which became septic, and suffered agonies until his arm was saved. Another time, a hammer driver was operating the wooden driving handle of the hammer when the band broke. The tension caused the handle to kick up, hitting the lad under the chin, breaking his jaw and throwing him in the air. He too was off work for a long time.

In peacetime most of our output was for the motor industry and its spin-offs – stampings for propellor shafts and gearboxes, hoists, carwashers, hydraulic jacks, and so on. Unlike the war years we were sometimes short of work. In November 1952, for instance, there were two drop hammers idle out of seven. We also had to cope with power shortages, power cuts and working staggered hours to make the best use of what power there was. Sometimes we would be starting work early in the morning and at other times beginning at midday and working until 8 pm.

Steel was another item in short supply and sometimes transport was the difficulty. I recollect one load of steel being lost on the railway for days. Our buyer, who was a witty and resourceful man, managed to get steel supplies in the form of railway waggon axles which, after Brinell and Izod tests, were found to be acceptable.

Several of us thought that when peace came the Stores Controller would leave to take up his former occupation again and peddle insurance. But our hopes were dashed and he remained a source of trouble like a wood splinter in your thumb.

One of our dropstampers was a tall, slim, handsome, fair-haired young man called Colin, a keen motorcyclist. In September 1951 he decided to go with some others to the races at Oliver's Mount, Scarborough. They were going by road. Colin had left his machine behind and was riding pillion on his brother-in-law's motorbike. I don't think people wore crash helmets much in those days but in this case it would have made no difference, for the brother-in-law was killed outright in a collision with a car near Driffield and Colin, who was catapulted for more than a hundred feet, died within a week. When he died the whole firm mourned for he was known everywhere and he had everything to live for – a happy marriage, a child just born; his death seemed so pointless. In October 1948 a glossy works magazine had come into existence and when Colin died in 1951 I paid tribute in its pages to one whom the Gods loved and who as we know die young.

During the magazine's existence I contributed an article or short story every month. My first was called 'October Garland' as it appeared in that month and linked up various events and persons both famous and infamous who were connected with October. Most of my articles were, as far as I can remember, on historical subjects. My short stories were not very good – I lacked imagination. I have found that one of my stories lingered in people's memories because I called my hero Denzil and the name amused them. It was after I had achieved a little minor celebrity with my magazine contributions that a man stopped me on the Machine Shop and asked me if I could provide a script for a pantomime to entertain the youngsters at the Christmas Party. I duly produced a script for Aladdin which seemed to please everybody. It was surprising what a lot of talent came to light in the factory, so much so that a concert party was formed that took our annual pantomime to places all over Sheffield raising money for charity and entertaining the handicapped. I had now become secretary as well as scriptwriter, but I think the success of the shows was due to having a good producer and a very good comedian in the Norman Evans/Widow Twanky tradition. He operated a milling machine in the factory but he was obviously a born comic. When he got his make-up and costume on he seemed to undergo a complete change of identity. His nickname 'Pea', pronounced 'Pay', became his stage name.

Church halls and a mental hospital were among the places we played in. The church halls had one thing in common, they were all cold and draughty and one place was infested with fleas. There was a hall we used regularly where as elsewhere the size of the audience was limited by fire regulations to a certain figure. When I arrived for the opening night at one of our last concerts, the producer dashed up with the alarming news that the fire brigade had insisted on the capacity of the hall being reduced by twenty seats. We had not been warned of this and the house was sold out for the same number of seats as formerly, so each performance was quite an ordeal. We expected that a fireman might turn up to inspect the hall and perhaps stop the performance. But we were lucky, nothing happened.

My journalism came to an end when the works magazine was discontinued as part of a cost-cutting exercise, and I began to lose interest in the concert party and pantomimes. After several successful years the concert party was disbanded. Pea, who had become well known in the areas in which we performed, returned to the Machine Shop, having shown us that he was not only a very good comic but a very nice man.

By 1953 lunch at the Waggon and Horses had gone up to 2s 6d, 2s 9d if one had soup. Looking back, it seems remarkable value. On 17 February the sole topic of conversation was the report that Derek Dooley, the darling of Owlerton, the red wonder of Sheffield Wednesday, had gangrene in his injured leg and that he was going to lose it. When Dooley lost his leg I had already worked nearly twenty years in the factory and at the same job. I was to work there for several more years and it didn't seem that there would ever be any change.

My loss of interest in the concert party was part of a wider feeling of loneliness, despair and disinterest that hung over me. For twenty years I had worked in the factory and at the same job; for a long time I had been content to look after my mother and think only of books, music and the other arts. I found that at work I was regarded as too useful where I was to be moved to any position better paid and above all pleasanter – not as noisy, dirty or hot. What would happen when Maurice retired I could not foresee, but within the company I saw no one I could work with.

The future seemed mapped out for me like an empty desert. I had reached an age when most men were married, some more than once, but I still remained single. I realized that I lacked the qualities that appealed to women, and I lacked also the money that for some women makes up for the absence of more glamorous qualities. My attempts to ingratiate myself with members of the other sex never seemed to come to anything and only caused me to feel pain, as if I had been burned, and led me to resolve not to be involved in what was not for me. Yet I longed to have someone with whom I could discuss everything and share everything.

Some people seek to impose their will on life and achieve their ambitions, some feel their life to be directed in a way from which there is no escape, and like me feel they are drifting down a river and all they can do is to accept whatever lies ahead. But I did know what I would like my destiny to be. Sometimes I prayed for it, but without hope – that I should no longer be an anonymous insect in the great city ant heap, but find myself in a village or small town where I was known as an individual human being.

# CHAPTER NINETEEN

# A NEW BEGINNING

In the last years of my life in the flats the council seemed to have a policy of not using the housing for family units. Most of them were now occupied by the old and the late middle-aged. The air-raid shelters were demolished at last and so was St James's church. The interior of the church had been burned out and the fittings were gone but the stone shell of the building was intact; restoration was possible, but the spirit of the time was against it. There was a great desire to sweep away the ruins of war – people wanted to forget the past. Then again, much of the population of the parish had been moved away and, most compelling reason of all, a lot of money could be raised by selling the site.

Demolition of Sheffield's only Georgian church proved a difficult job. The builders had done their work well. Beneath the church the crypt housed iron coffins containing the remains of the professional and business classes, merchants, lawyers and architects. The coffins, which had been made in Manchester, had to be emptied for reburial at Wardsend. I was told by a reliable source that the police surgeon was called to view the perfectly preserved body of a pretty young girl with long blonde hair.

My local bookshop, Hartley Seed, was bought by Armstrong Duffield, a bright, lively, fair-haired young man and I remember seeing him talking to Mr Seed, a white-haired old gentleman with a high collar, a perfect example of old-style business integrity. Almost immediately after this, Mr Duffield suffered a cruel fate. He was struck down by poliomyelitis, which was then a great scourge, but he and his wife kept the business going. From my window I could see him being pushed in a wheelchair to the Golden Ball at lunch time.

Cadmans bookshop, which in my childhood had occupied one of a row of shops on the site of the City Hall, had then taken new premises in one of a row of shops just past the Royal Hospital. While Cadmans sold new books, the great delight for bookworms was their enormous stock of secondhand books – every wall was covered with shelf upon shelf of books, tables groaned under the weight of books, stacks of books were everywhere and great care was needed in picking one's way round the shop. Everything was covered in dust. Mr Duffield purchased the shop; I don't know if many bargains were to be found among the stock. Very soon it reopened under the name of Hartley Seed, bright, well-organized, clean, full of the latest publications. It was a much more convenient shop to browse in, but the thrill of finding the unexpected had gone.

There were other changes. The blacksmith's shop near the old synagogue on Silver Street Head was demolished in February 1952 and in November of the same year Waterhouses pork shop on West Bar changed hands; this was a shop which had been part of the landscape since my earliest days.

Rationing continued for years after the war, but supplies gradually improved. Now, in the day of the Common Market and the multinational companies, I remember with incredulity the prices one paid in the decade after the war. In October 1948 we paid £73 10s for a proper white stone memorial on the family grave in which granny, one of her sisters, and my uncle George William were buried. Now that our fortunes had improved slightly we bought a kitchen table in August 1953 for £17 3s 8d, a dressing table in August 1953 for 13 guineas and a three-piece suite in March 1954 for £45. Most men had a wet shave in those days, and in February 1949 I bought myself a new shaving brush for 7s 4d; I got myself a pair of black boots for £2 13s 4d in October 1952, and in April 1953 I obtained a raincoat for £2 10s from The Raincoat Shop which then flourished in Orchard Street, the site now covered by the splendours of Orchard Square. From today's world of our metricated and Europeanized coinage the cost of food and household goods expressed in the old Anglo-Saxon money seems almost trivial, with boiled ham at 1s 10d a quarter pound, Marks & Spencer's Irish fruit cake at 2s 9d a pound, a bottle of port at 18s, ammonia at 9d a bottle and a hair cut at 1s 6d.

On 14 July 1951 I agreed to buy a 10 inch Marconi television set from Cockaynes; it was priced at £48 but like most poor people we bought it on terms, on 'the never' as it was called, so it cost us more, and the licence was another £2. It was in 1951 that TV reached Sheffield, but in our case we didn't actually have a picture until October, when we were just in time to see the closing ceremonies of the Festival of Britain. We had several of our neighbours in to watch the new wonder with us and we kept open house for weeks, as we were to do again at the time of the Coronation.

The author, *c.* 1948

A few days after we started viewing a man came from the Town Hall and said we must have the aerial taken down. It was secured to the chimney stack on the roof and it put the stack in danger. I could not believe this, for the chimney stacks on the flats are massive brick structures not unlike mile castles on the Roman Wall. I consulted with such people as I knew who already had TV and other experts in this new field and I was relieved to find that they dismissed any possibility of damage to the stacks with incredulity and even mirth.

Aware that my views as an individual would carry no weight with the civic bureaucracy I went to see our managing director, who was a City Councillor. He was very kind, listened sympathetically to my story and telephoned a high official in the Town Hall to whom he said that our television set was bringing 'a little sunshine into an old lady's life'. Whoever he spoke to, the effect was immediate, the objections were withdrawn and we heard nothing more, and in fact although we were the first to have TV on the flats we were by no means the last.

I do not feel triumphant now when I think how TV has squeezed out so much entertainment, instruction and social life that we then enjoyed. Films were better, more plentiful, and available in nearby cinemas. The live variety theatre was still truly alive, the circus came to town more than once and in March 1953 Chipperfields Circus marched in procession to the Big Top in Devonshire Street, passing our flats on the way.

In the flats the number of people we knew continued to diminish. In January 1952 the elder of the two Irish sisters who lived next to us died. Ellen had been failing for a long time and was little but skin and bone when she passed away. She had a sweet nature. Her sister, Ada, was comforted by the companionship of her two cats; she was deaf but in April she was saying she heard people singing hymns in the street at 4 am. Despite this aberration, she was to live her lonely life for several more years. We also lost the Catholic widow who had succeeded Miss Sally in the top flat; when she first came she had a little one-eyed Pekinese called Congo, she used to say it was like having a child in the house. In February 1953 the shopkeeper of the half-moon shop died; the worries of coping with rationing almost certainly shortened his life.

About a month later neighbours called the police to the groundfloor flat in Campo Lane where the mother of my friend Albert had continued to live after her husband left her. She had not been seen for a number of days and it was thought she was dead, but when they broke in she was alive and seemed quite unconcerned by the commotion. She had lost all sense of hearing. During the war bombs and alerts never broke through her screen of silence; only her disagreeable job in a hide and skin warehouse kept her in touch with the outside world. Her son Albert came back from the army and people said he had been lucky, for he never went outside the UK and practised his own trade of joinery in the army. His luck seemed to continue, he got a job and he got a prefab at Sky Edge to house himself, his young wife and two children. Then things changed; he was struck down by an incurable disease and became bedridden, needing constant attention; then both children were found to be suffering from asthma. Most wives would look to their mother-in-law for help, but Albert's mother had sunk into a state of semi-consciousness. She probably never understood that her son was ill, as she slept from life to death; when the police broke in a second time she was dead, and her son would follow her.

The Townhead Street Flats following modernization, in 1965

'Look to the end' were the words, in Herodotus, of a philosopher asked to marvel at the wealth and good fortune of the King of Lydia. Like Croesus my childhood friend Young Tom and his parents seemed destined to a bright future after his teacher took his career in hand. Gradually the picture changed. The teacher took over the role of father. Young Tom married a girl who seemed to despise his parents. Then the teacher died and left most of his property to Young Tom so that he and his wife were able to move to a favoured district of Sheffield. Although Young Tom served overseas he returned unscathed, as it seemed, to his new home. His father died and he visited his mother from time to time and she was able to rejoice in his success in becoming the art master at a large grammar school. Then suddenly he was struck down by a tumour on the brain which first blinded him and then killed him. He left his wife and daughter well provided for — his mother not at all, nor was it the widow's intention to keep in contact with her.

This seemed a tragic end to the story — but wait, there may be a happy ending, there usually is in fiction. Several years later when we called on Tommy's mother we found Grace not only cheerful as she always was but filled with a new spirit of optimism. Her granddaughter, now a teenager, had called to see her and stayed for tea. They had enjoyed their conversation and on leaving the girl had said how pleased she was to have got to know her father's mother, and that she would soon call again. This could be the start of a beautiful relationship, as the grandmother could see the dead son in his daughter's qualities, but this isn't fiction. There is no happy ending. The granddaughter never called again. 'I suppose she just wanted to see what I looked like!' Grace said without bitterness when months had gone by and it was evident the girl was not going to come. The daughter-in-law remained aloof, although Young Tom's success had been due in great measure to his mother's willingness to give up her home and act as housekeeper to his teacher. Grace died in 1976, bedridden and alone, having outlived nearly all her friends and relatives and left her body for medical research. In her case her body had worn out but her mind remained clear to the end.

From the beginning of the Great War to the end of the Second, our friend who had been in charge of the usherettes at the Albert Hall and thanks to whom granny and my mother had gained the job of washing towels and so forth used by the staff, had been a source of help and advice to all her neighbours. She seemed such a calm, sensible, friendly woman that when after the war a change came over her it was not only a shock but at first it seemed a trifling matter; after all a failing memory is common to many people as they grow old. In her case she became really silly, everything was a laughing matter. She had the only flat in the building still using gas for everything including lighting and she was continually turning on her gas appliances and forgetting to light them. Her neighbours feared an explosion but she found it all very funny. Everyone said the change in her was due to worry about her husband, the large solid ex-policeman who had been transformed into a vegetable by a stroke, and above all the worry of finding the money to keep him in a private mental hospital.

When the war ended we heard again of Miss Minnie who had lived in the top flat and who had longed to return to India where she had been born. During the war years she had worked as a missionary in Jamaica. Now it seemed her time had come and she went as a missionary to an area near Trichinopoly in south India, but a circumstance arose which she had not foreseen. It was essential that she learn the language of the area but although she applied herself to learning it her age was against her; she made slow progress and after a time she had to return to England, her dream shattered. She was so kind to me as a child, kindling my love of books, that I always longed to see her again but she died in October 1973 without us having that last meeting.

A few years after the end of the war we saw a notice in the evening paper announcing the death of my father. He had been living in a block of flats in the Park district. I think they had been erected by private enterprise and were built of brick and of modest size, not like the multi-storey monsters that would soon be springing up. After visiting my father's last habitation I began to think for the first time that he was not a villain but a victim and now I feel my mother was too weak. She allowed granny to live her life and in the process ruin those of my parents and to some extent my own. The only thing I acquired as a result of my father's death was a photograph of him in his watchman's uniform in one of the Sheffield Markets, with his dog.

The face of Sheffield was changing. I had been one of the early babies to be born in our flats, only a few years after they were built. For so long they had formed a community in themselves, but now their own future was no longer certain. Those who had shared so many years of our lives had died or moved away.

I have said that at one time I had regarded myself as being 'without luck'. In spite of that I had had a full share in the working and cultural life of the city; there was only one aspect of life in which I had not found at least some fulfilment. I foresaw a lonely, celibate life before me and very likely not a very long one.

When 1953 began it seemed as if it would be a year in the familiar pattern into which my life had evolved. Apart from work, books, radio and now television, I went to musical events and theatres, and visited art galleries and museums – always alone and with a growing sensation of emptiness. There was no one to confide in, or share the thoughts that seemed to well up from time to time. I had no relatives in Sheffield except my mother, and such as I had elsewhere were remote figures who had no common interest with me. Sometimes at exhibition and concerts I would try to achieve contact with a woman by starting a conversation, but it would lead to nothing. Yet although I did not know it a profound change was about to take place that would break the mould in which my life was set.

Abraham Cowley's poem *The Wish* had always chimed in with my own desires, but I never thought that the wish expressed by the poet in the second verse would be answered in my case.

Ah, yet, e'er I descend to th' Grave
May I a small house, and a large Garden have!
And a few Friends and many Books, both true,
Both wise and both delightful too!
And since Love ne'er will from me flee,
A Mistress moderately fair,
And good as Guardian Angels are
Only beloved, and loving me.

In the years 1947, 1948 and 1949 my mother and I had gone on coach tours – the last of them to London – but now in 1953 it looked as if we wouldn't be able to risk going away from home as she was turned 70. On 12 April, getting up in the morning, mother fell and broke her thigh. Our doctor got her in the Royal Infirmary where they operated on her. I had never been to this hospital before, the first to be opened in Sheffield at the beginning of the nineteenth century. Unlike the Royal Hospital, which was built straight up from the pavement, the Infirmary had extensive grounds; at the time I didn't take much notice that the Georgian building was obscured in places by later additions. In the same ward as mother was a girl called Anne.

After a few days, mother was transferred to Wharncliffe Hospital for convalescence. It meant me catching a bus to the Wisewood estate on the north-western side of the city when I visited her. A short walk from the bus terminus brought me to the gate of the hospital and here a rather steep drive led down to a series of wooden huts housing the wards. It was quite a pleasant situation although it could be bleak; the whole complex had been a hospital for war wounded in the Great War.

The first time I visited Wharncliffe, mother said how pleased she was that Anne had also been moved there, and indicated a teenage girl in a bed on the other side of the ward. Anne was a real live wire, mother said, in and out of bed all the time, up and down helping the nurses despite a stiff leg that she could not bend. The young girl had two visitors, a white-haired old gentleman and a handsome fresh-faced woman who looked to be a country type. As I watched them the old gentleman produced a horseshoe and the three of them put their heads together and examined it. 'Oh!' I thought, 'I see what's happened! The girl has had a riding accident, and the shoe belongs to her horse!' I often look at strangers and imagine what their background must be, but in this case I was wildly wrong.

Anne suffered from osteomyelitis, a bone disease that flared up from time to time, when surgery was needed to remove infected bone, and she had never ridden a horse. The horseshoe was only a good-luck symbol. The fresh-faced woman was Anne's mother, Sally, and was a regular visitor. She came across the ward to exchange a few words with us from time to time. She said that the family lived in a village in Derbyshire in an old stone house, and named the village, but I had no idea where it was. 'Near Killamarsh,' she said, and suddenly I remembered seeing that name on a small shabby red bus parked in a side street off the Moor at the end of the war.

The coronation of the new queen was one of our topics of conversation, and the fact that the ceremony was going to be shown on television for the first time made it more exciting. It was evident that mother was going to be at Wharncliffe until after the date of the coronation and I expected her to be disappointed at missing seeing it on our new set, but no, she was reconciled to staying in hospital. Every ward, she told me, was going to have a big screen on which an enlarged picture would be projected. The ward had become a familiar world to her and I looked forward to my weekend visits and the return when I could escort my new friend, Anne's mother, to the bus and back to Sheffield.

In conversation I discovered that her younger brother worked at the same firm at Millhouses as I did, although I only knew him by sight. We found that we had quite a number of common interests, so I was sorry when I heard that her daughter was being discharged and was going home. This meant there would be no more chats on the bus and my friend would fade into the past. She too seemed sorry that our brief contact would be at an end. I thought of one of my favourite quotations from an Indian poem, 'As a log floating on the waters meets another log so do men meet and part again.' So I thought this too is just an episode.

When we reached Sheffield at the end of her last visit to Wharncliffe we stopped to talk and she said that when my mother had recovered we ought to visit her and her family in Derbyshire. As we spoke, a strange thought entered my mind. This handsome, accomplished woman was not just making polite noises, she really liked me. Then a surge of desire swept over me, to be followed by the fear that I might be mistaken. Could this be the chance of happiness I never thought would come, the companion with whom I could share all? And if it was that chance, how easily I could lose it!

On the day of the coronation I had the living-room of our flat full of friends and neighbours. I ought to have said 'friends who were neighbours also'. I had warned them that I would be going to Wharncliffe in the afternoon, to share the rest of the event with my mother. The warm, cosy flat, the ancient, glittering ceremonies, the company of my friends, obscured the cold, wet, cheerless reality of the weather outside. Stepping out into the deserted streets, I caught an empty bus to Wisewood. When I reached my mother's ward the broadcast was still in full swing with all the dignitaries making their way from the Abbey in the rain. In the ward it was rather like Christmas, with people sharing goodies, a crowd of visitors and staff watching the huge screen and through the windows a very dark winter sky.

It was not until 20 June that mother left hospital and it was a while before it seemed wise to take up my new friend's invitation to visit her. Eventually we agreed on a date and I hired a taxi to take us. We had been given instructions that the house we were to visit was at a crossroads on the A616. We duly reached what we thought was the crossroads and passed through before our driver halted. We looked round to get our bearings and check with someone. It was very quiet, there was only an occasional vehicle. On all sides there were trees; on the left side of the road where we had come to a stop could be seen a wide meadow behind a group of chestnut trees. On the right, trees formed a black screen that, as we realized later, prevented us from seeing the rectory.

With relief we saw a lady approaching us – she was gathering plants of some sort. We told her the name of the house we were looking for and she waved her hand to the right.

'Brook House!' she said.

'Oh no,' I said, 'that is not the name, it is Brookfield.'

'Oh, you mean the old house.' She gestured to the left where we could just make out a building behind some trees.

This was indeed the house we were seeking and my friend was standing by a rather dilapidated wooden gate which she opened for us. As we entered a figure like Father Time came to join her, bearing a massive scythe on his shoulder; this was her father, whom we had seen at Wharncliffe.

It was a large house. There was a tall stone part with a roof of massive stone tiles, and joined to it, crouching like a poor relation, was what was evidently an older house with a mullioned window and a red-tiled roof. We entered through a massive wooden door opening onto a long corridor. Accustomed to our modest flat, everything seemed to us on an enormous scale and it looked as if it would be easy to lose one's way in such a house.

We spent most of our time in an enormous front room which we were told had been flooded twenty years before. We enjoyed our visit and we went again at Christmas, to a family party at Brookfield. Anne was the youngest of three children. She had two brothers a little older than herself and each more than six feet tall.

My friend, their mother Sally, had very deceptively good looks – she could easily have passed herself off as an older sister. It was inevitable that I should fall in love with her – she was such fun to be with and liked so many of the things I liked, and having had a rural background was able to introduce me to pleasures I had never known.

It was unfortunate that what should have been a period of unalloyed happiness was also a period of great pain and misery. My mother had liked Sally and the rest of her family, but as soon as she realized what was happening her attitude changed. She stormed and raged. She was a very stubborn woman and all the assurances in the world made no impression on her. It was a very painful period in my life, although the more I got to know Sally the more I realized she was the one for me.

At the end of 1954 Sally and I were married and I left the city to live with her at Brookfield, only visiting the flats after that to care for my mother every Saturday and Sunday, shopping and doing other jobs for her. Her heart may have been affected by her distress at the change in our lives, because after a time she collapsed and was taken to hospital; while there she died in her sleep.

My last link was broken, my life was now elsewhere, but I shall always be a Sheffielder.